TWAYNE'S WORLD AUTHORS SERIES

A Survey of the World's Literature

Sylvia E. Bowman, Indiana University

GENERAL EDITOR

SPAIN

Gerald E. Wade, Vanderbilt University

EDITOR

Ana María Matute

(TWAS 152)

TWANYE'S WORLD AUTHOR SERIES (TWAS)

The purpose of TWAS is to survey the major writers—novelists, dramatists, historians, poets, philosophers, and critics—of the nations of the world. Among the national literatures covered are those of Australia, Canada, China, Eastern Europe, France, Germany, Greece, India, Italy, Japan, Latin America, New Zealand, Poland, Russia, Scandinavia, Spain, and the African nations, as well as Hebrew, Yiddish, and Latin Classical literatures. This survey is complemented by Twayne's United States Authors Series and English Authors Series.

The intent of each volume in these series is to present a critical-analytical study of the works of the writer; to include biographical and historical material that may be necessary for understanding, appreciation, and critical appraisal of the writer; and to present all material in clear, concise English—but not to vitiate the scholarly content of the work by doing so.

ANA MARÍA MATUTE

By JANET DÍAZ
University of North Carolina

Twayne Publishers, Inc.   : :   New York

To Julita

Preface

Ana María Matute is one of Spain's three or four most important novelists of the post-Civil War period (1939 to the present). Critics are nearly unanimous in considering her the leading woman novelist in Spain today, and many suggest that she is the best woman novelist now writing in Spanish. The intent of this book is to present her life and works to the general English-speaking public, on a level hopefully meaningful at once to the high school student and professional Hispanist. Simultaneously, attention is given the culture and atmosphere in which her works were produced. Spain's more or less traditional isolation from the rest of Europe, deliberately intensified for a time by the Franco regime, has created numerous obstacles to the diffusion of Spanish literature beyond the national boundaries, with writers and works of prime importance at times remaining unknown for years to the world at large. This situation is slowly changing, having begun significantly to do so in the decade of the sixties. The Spanish Civil War (1936—1939), paradoxically, may have helped, despite the immediate negative effects, for it served to draw the attention of other nations to Spain, dramatically underscoring how little was really known of conditions there.

It may be partly because of her almost inseparable association with themes of the Civil War that Matute has roused a special interest in other countries, scoring notable successes in translation. With her novels rendered to every Western European tongue except Greek, and having also appeared in several "Iron Curtain" languages, Matute has achieved a foreign exposure and acceptance which is neither easy nor frequent for Spanish writers. This is further attested by several American translations and editions, and lecture tours.

Ana María Matute appeared on the Spanish novelistic scene in 1948 with the publication of *Los Abel (The Abel Family)*, but did not emerge as a major figure until a decade later, when her monumental novel of the Civil War, *Los hijos muertos (The Dead Children)*, was awarded the Spanish Critics' Prize as the best novel of 1958, and shortly afterward obtained the National Literary Prize, "Miguel de Cervantes." The three volumes of her trilogy, *Los mercaderes (The Merchants)*, which began appearing in 1960, have been considered individually and collectively as major literary events, with some critics suggesting that the trilogy is the most significant literary entity of the postwar period in Spain.

In interviews, lectures, and autobiographical sketches, Matute has repeatedly emphasized the importance of certain experiences of her early years, particularly the exposure to the Castilian countryside and peasants, and the emotional impact of the Civil War, which broke out when she was ten years old. Because both the Castilian countryside and the Civil War are frequent and obsessive themes in her writing, it seemed necessary to give unusually detailed attention to her childhood experiences with them, as they are obviously related closely to the content and comprehension of her work. Biographical data are not included simply for their own sake, but when they aid the understanding and evaluation of the literary product. I have attempted to indicate where appropriate the relevance of biographical background to specific characters and events, and to show to what degree Matute makes use of autobiographical materials in her works, although it is clear always that she has done much more than simply to reproduce personal experience.

Matute's work is sufficiently recent that there is only a limited amount of secondary material available, and much of this is either of little value or is inaccessible (by far the majority of articles about her appeared in Spanish newspapers). The peculiar nature of Spanish criticism must also be considered, for that produced within the country is often politically motivated, for better or for worse, and must be discounted accordingly. The situation is further complicated by the existence of the censorship, affecting not only the primary literature, but critical evaluations. If certain aspects of a work have escaped the censors, the critic does the author a considerable disservice by calling attention to this fact. Therefore, much contemporary Spanish criticism is either superficial, or so cautiously worded as to be almost incomprehensible to the uninitiated. I have consequently relied mainly on French and English criticisms of Matute when available, and since these are so few in number that it would be abusive to cite them often, the overwhelming majority of critical judgments are entirely my own. The same is true of translations from Matute's work or other sources to English, unless otherwise indicated. I have worked almost exclusively with the original texts. Translations are kept to a minimum because Matute's lyric, personal style suffers greatly upon rendering into another language, and no translation, however polished, seems to do justice to the tone of the original. In order to compensate, I have discussed in somewhat greater detail the content and import of the various works, preserving as much as possible the flavor and emotion of Matute, and attempting to convey her "message" and general atmosphere by means other than extensive textual citations.

La torre vigía (The Watchtower), Matute's most recent work to date, was published when the present study was in the final stages of publication and is included only in the chronology. Preliminary examination indicates that it differs in significant aspects from her writing heretofore, such as its temporal exoticism (set in the Middle Ages), in the style deliberately sprinkled with archaic flavorings, and the numerous chivalric motifs. However, other constants found in Matute's earlier narratives remain: concentration on the child and adolescent character, the solitude and alienation of the protagonist, criticism of materialistic values and of violence, and just beneath the surface, a strong critique of Spain's social system, here shown to have been just as beset with problems and tensions in its beginnings as it is today. The new elements, considered in addition to the notable evolution in her publications of this decade, strongly suggest further changes in the novelist's future development, and indicate the rashness of pretending to write the "final word" on Matute at this date.

During the preparation of this study, I was fortunate to be able to examine the unique collection of Matute juvenilia and unpublished manuscripts which the novelist donated in 1965 to the Mogar Library of Boston University. This material is almost completely unknown to scholars, and is often particularly illuminating of the novelist's personality and works, and especially revealing of the origin or longevity of certain constant themes and preoccupations. I am grateful to the library staff and to Dr. Howard Gottlieb for their assistance and patience in my use of this collection. Thanks are due also to Ana María Matute for her kindness and cooperation.

CONTENTS

Chronology

1926 July 26: Born, Barcelona, Spain.

1930 Near death during prolonged illness.

1934 Serious illnesses, lasting until following year; sent after first illness to live in country for profoundly important convalescence.

1936 July 18: Outbreak of Civil War; family confined to house. Founds a children's magazine.

1939 Fall of Republican Government in March. Returns to school.

1941 Abandons formal education to write, study painting and violin.

1942 "El Chico de al lado," ("The Boy Next Door") appears in *Destino*.

1943 Music and painting abandoned for exclusive dedication to writing. Works on *Pequeño teatro (Little Theater)*.

1945 Writing of *Los Abel (The Abel Family)*.

1947 *Los Abel* in competition for Premio Nadal is named finalist.

1948 Publication of *Los Abel*, "official" beginning of novelistic career.

1951 First literary prize, "Tertulia Café del Turia," for short story, "No hacer nada" ("Doing Nothing"). *Infidele alla terra*, Italian translation of *Los Abel*, published in November. Begins *Los hijos muertos (The Dead Children)*.

1952 *Fiesta al noroeste (Celebration in the Northwest)* is completed, awarded Premio Café Gijón. Marries Ramón Eugenio de Goicoechea in November.

1954 Birth of son, Juan Pablo. Corrected version of *Pequeño teatro* wins Premio Planeta and is published.

1955 *En esta tierra (In This Land)*, rewritten version of censored novel, *Las luciérnagas (The Fireflies)* is published.

1956 "Los cuentos, vagabundos" ("Vagabond Stories"). *Los niños tontos (The Stupid Children)*. Enters field of juvenile fiction with *El país de la pizarra (Blackboard Land)*.

1957 *El tiempo (Time)*, collected short stories, is published.

1958 *Los hijos muertos* is published and wins Spanish Critics' prize as best novel of the year.

1959 *Los hijos muertos* is awarded National Literary Prize, "Miguel de Cervantes." Matute receives 50,000 pesetas from Fundación March to work on trilogy, *Los mercaderes (The Merchants).*

1960 *Primera memoria (First memoirs),* first volume of the trilogy, wins Premio Nadal and publication. Matute becomes corresponding member of Hispanic Society of America. *Paulina, el mundo y las estrellas (Pauline, the World and the Stars),* novel for adolescent girls and *El saltamontes verde (The Green Grasshopper),* children's fiction. French translations of *El tiempo (Le temps)* and *Primera memoria (Les brûlures du matin).*

1961 *El arrepentido (The Repentant One).* collected short stories. *Libro de juegos para los niños de los otros (Book of Games for the Others' Children). Historias de la Artámila (Tales of Artamila). Tres y un sueño (Three [Fantasies] and a Dream). A la mitad del camino (Halfway down the Road).* First visit to Paris. *Fiesta al noroeste* translated to French and Italian, *Primera memoria* to Portuguese, and *Los niños tontos* to German.

1962 *Caballito loco (Little Crazy Horse),* children's stories. *Pequeño teatro* appears in French *(Marionettes).*

1963 January: Definitive separation from husband. Travels in Greece, Corfu, France, Belgium, Germany, Switzerland. *El río (The River). Plaignez les loups,* French translation of *Los hijos muertos.* English and American editions of *Primera memoria.*

1964 *Los soldados lloran de noche (The Soldiers Cry By Night),* Second volume of trilogy, *Los mercaderes.* First visit to United States in autumn, lecturing at several Universities.

1965 *El polizón del "Ulises" (The Cabin Boy of the "Ulysses")* awarded Premio Lazarillo, national prize for children's literature. Legally separated from husband; wins custody of son. Extensive travel in Scandinavia, Northern and Central Europe. Returns to United States in fall as Visiting Professor at University of Indiana.

1966 Returns to Barcelona; lectures in various Spanish cities.

1968 Fixes residence in Sitges. *Algunos muchachos (A Few Kids),* collected short stories.

1969 Visiting Professor at University of Oklahoma during first months of year. Lectures at various southern and western universities. *La trampa (The Trap),* third volume of trilogy, *Los mercaderes.*

1971 Fined 50,000 pesetas for role in drafting and signing of "Montserrat Manifesto" in December of 1970. *La torre vigía (The Watchtower),* social variant of "chivalric" novel.

CHAPTER 1

The Formative Years

A NUMBER of Matute's works shed light on her background, childhood, and significant experiences. Especially important in this respect are the collection of so-called chronicles, *A la mitad del camino (Halfway Down the Road)*, the memoirs, *El río (The River)* and several short stories, most of which are found in *Historias de la Artámila (Tales of Artámila)*. In addition, the novelist has given numerous interviews to Spanish and foreign journalists whose questions seem to have emphasized primarily her early life. Thus, a large percentage of the available articles are autobiographical in nature, dealing with her life before her marriage. Since these usually appeared in newspapers, however, this material is of rather difficult access. Then, too, it must be noted that Matute has spoken much less freely of her adult life. The scholar slowly becomes aware that the apparent wealth of informative articles is repetitive and limited, and that the seemingly communicative writer has actually been quite reticent about her personal history, with the exception of a few early years and key experiences obsessively emphasized.

I   *The Settings*

Three areas, three widely different and contrasting scenes, frame the early years of Ana María Matute. Their formative influence is strong, and is easily discernible in her writing. She is usually considered to be from Barcelona, where she was born, but her first ten years were almost equally divided between that city, Madrid, and the remote mountain village of Mansilla de la Sierra, near the border between Old Castile and Navarre.

Barcelona, capital of the province of Catalonia on the northern Mediterranean coast, is Spain's largest city and most important industrial center. As such, it was one of a very few Spanish centers to develop a fairly well-defined proletariat; as the manufacturing center, it claims much of the industrial bourgeoisie and the small middle class. Catalonia, rich agriculturally as well as industrially, has perennially resented supporting other regions of Spain, and its strong independent and separatist spirit has frequently led to conflict with the central government. Barcelona, port and metropolis, is traditionally a center not only of trade, but of change, of social and political ferment, all of which give a peculiar, indelible violence to its intervention in the Civil War. This conflict, witnessed and endlessly recalled in Barcelona, is ever present (implicitly or explicitly) in Matute's work.

There is a long-standing rivalry between Madrid and Barcelona, and a somewhat traditional hostility between residents of the two regions. Intellectual competition is also keen. Barcelona as a cultural and literary center is second to Madrid in the number of writers in residence, but probably claims a larger share of the liberal or "opposition" writers than the capital. The contrast between the two cities is strong: Madrid's climate is harsher than that of Barcelona, and its surroundings lack the geographical beauty of the seaport. The central plateau near Madrid is barren and flat, a sea of dust in summer and of mud in winter. Its landscape is desert-like, the bare, brown earth dominated by the sky and wind. The city itself, an artificially created seat of government in the geographical center of the country, is not self-sustaining but dependent on necessities brought from outside. Relatively new among Spanish cities (it is a scant four centuries old), its massive buildings reflect its bureaucratic nature, and something of the austerity of the surrounding landscape. This atmosphere seems to have been alien to Matute even as a child, and her youthful dislike only intensified during her residence there after her marriage. Despite its undeniable charms for others, this city has always depressed her, and as an adult she avoids it whenever possible. This feeling is perhaps unconsciously projected in her work, inasmuch as both Barcelona and Mansilla have served repeatedly as settings for her fiction, but not a single one of her narratives takes place in Madrid.

The word "matute" in Spanish means "contraband," but nothing indicates that the novelist's ancestors derived their surname from this activity. They were rural gentry, originally from the north central plateau of Old Castile, with strong roots in the country. The maternal grandparents lived on a country estate where Matute's mother was raised, in the rugged mountain range called Sierra de Cameros, between Burgos, Soria, and Logroño. It is some twenty-five miles from Nájera, one-time royal residence of the kings of Navarre, and near the scene of events which shaped medieval Spanish history. Today Mansilla is well off the main highways, but centuries ago it was not far from the pilgrims' way to Santiago de Campostela. The entire area is strewn with shrines, monasteries, abbeys, hermitages, and historic churches. The area's early history also offers an example of war and violence between brothers, an instance of the Cain and Abel relationship so important in Matute's writing: Nájera in 1367 was the site of a bloody battle fought by Peter the Cruel and his illegitimate half-brother, Henry of Trastamara, with the former being assassinated shortly after by the latter.

Mansilla is reached by a secondary road from Nájera, the nearest town of any size, but is itself small, dusty, and antique, with small, fortress-like stone houses, and the characteristic ruined castle on a hill above. The balconies still bear carved coats-of-arms, draped by drying laundry on washdays. The road to Mansilla, lined with the black poplars so frequently mentioned by the novelist, follows·the clear stream of the Najerilla River, becoming narrow and winding as it climbs upward between the Sierra de la Demanda on the right hand, and the Sierra de Cameros, on the left. The valley narrows, becoming so steep that in places it is little more than a gorge, with occasional patches of cultivable land. In the mountains near Mansilla is situated a famous monastery founded by St. Millán in the sixth century, a center of religious and military resistance in the Moorish invasion. Rebuilt in the sixteenth century in the style of Herrera, architect of the Escorial, the building is so imposing and rich in art that it is called the "Escorial de la Rioja," Rioja being the name of this wine-producing region.

Just off the road lies the abbey of Valvanera, shrine of the area's patroness Virgin, reflected at least twice in Matute's writing, in the name of the protagonist-narrator of her first published novel, and a sketch in *El río (The River)* which recalls how monks of the abbey once supplied the area with chocolate made in their own kitchens. It was in the village of Mansilla that the novelist's family spent their summers, which were sometimes rather extended, as fall classes do not resume in Spain until October or November. The family resided alternately in Madrid and Barcelona during the rest of the year, because of the father's business. The contrast between the mountain village and the cities is, even today, difficult to imagine. Many rural areas of Old Castile are essentially unchanged since the Middle Ages. Most villages are unpaved, without electricity, often reached only on foot or horseback. The appearance of the buildings, the manner of dress, the general patterns of life and customs have long since vanished in most of Europe, but in Spain, even in relatively accessible areas, farmers may still be seen using the agricultural methods of two thousand years ago. Grain is still threshed, as in biblical times, by the hooves of donkeys on the hard earth. In villages such as Matute knew as a child, the peasants still live in a sort of serfdom and in the most primitive conditions. Clothes are washed in what may be the area's only river and source of water. Isolation is extreme; the outside world, even the next village, is remote and unreal. News of the world, arriving late if at all, has little urgency for the villagers. Matute recalls in "Diarios atrasados" ("Old Newspapers") a sketch in *The River,* that when her family returned to the city at summer's end her father would be visited by a procession of elderly villagers asking for back issues of papers to read during the long, harsh winter. At the mercy of Castile's severe and capricious climate, the small farmer or sharecropper faces an unremitting battle with the rocky, infertile soil, living at best only on the survival level. These people, and particularly the shepherds and herdsmen, often live little better than animals. Whether for this reason, or because of the overwhelming economic importance of a cow or horse, Castilian peasants often show a special love for their animals, as recorded in various sections of Matute's memoirs.

Poverty is very much in evidence, and even if there were no wealthy people in the villages, the sensitive young future novelist would no doubt have soon become aware of social inequities. The typical village, however, includes a wealthy family or two, perhaps the closed palace and idle lands of an absent nobleman, while tenant farmers work most of their lives for a distant landlord. In the microcosm of the village, such contrasts are most striking, and thus the existence of social injustice impressed itself upon Matute from childhood.

II   *The Family and the Child*

Ana María Matute Ausejo was born on July 26, 1926, the second of five children of a Catalan industrialist. Her father was the owner of an umbrella factory; her mother was the "classic middle-class Spanish wife," educated exclusively for marriage and motherhood, whose world consisted of her home. Marriage within the family relationship has been practiced for centuries on certain social levels in Spain, and Matute's parents were distant relatives, her father being an uncle, three times removed, of her mother. The family was conservative, and the three girls and two boys received a traditional religious upbringing. It was a family without literary or artistic antecedents, with little intellectual life in the home. There was, however, a special closeness and affection between parents and children, and their family relationship seems to have been particularly happy. Few references to Matute's mother are to be found in her memoirs or the short stories drawing upon personal experience, but a number of anecdotes involve her father. Some of these illustrate his attitude toward children, not merely his own, but those of the village, indicating a gift for communication with the young. Many of Matute's stories of children reflect a warm, happy home life, and the majority of unhappy children about whom she writes are orphans. True, she also portrays misunderstood, problem-ridden children and adolescents, unable to communicate with the adult world, but there is no real reason to believe in an autobiographical basis. The novelist has stressed the pleasant memories of her early years, describing them with glowing adjectives, so that notes of melancholy and pessimism in her work are not traceable to an unhappy home or childhood.

Barcelona is an ancient city, whose heart reflects its antiquity in its ruined Roman walls, with the superimposed constructions of later centuries; or narrow and winding streets, often impassable for automobiles, and buildings crowded together haphazardly. The newer part of the city, the "Ensanche" (widening), was constructed when expansion in the last century forced demolition of the old walls. The new area follows a symmetrical division into blocks, with wide, straight streets stretching away from the port and narrow coastal plain into the low mountains. Toward the edge of this area, in a section which before the Civil War must have been suburban, the Matute family lived, in a pleasant, quiet neighborhood with a view of the city below and the Mediterranean beyond. The family still owns an apartment here in the short, shady street, Calle Platón, with its minimum of traffic and its peaceful air. Its atmosphere is rather far removed from the "Other Barcelona" below, the port, slums, and famous vice district, with the fringes of the underworld crowded in together with the historical and picturesque.

While not an invalid, as a child Matute's health was delicate; she suffered prolonged and serious illnesses at the ages of four, eight, and nine. On the first occasion, she hovered near death with complications of a kidney infection, and despite her tender age seems to have had some awareness of the danger. This experience, with the subsequent long confinement of convalescence, apparently caused her to withdraw more deeply into that world of fantasy in which all children live to some degree. The novelist has frequently mentioned the importance of illusion in her childhood, and has given us an excellent description of what her imaginary world must have been like in the opening paragraphs of "Los niños buenos" ("The Good Children"), one of the stories in the collection *El tiempo (Time)*.

Sometimes I think how much I would like to travel through a child's mind. From what I remember of my own childhood, I think it must have a certain resemblance to the palette of a mad painter; a chaotic land of variegated and undisciplined colors, wherein lie an infinity of brilliant islands, red lagoons, coasts with human profiles, dark cliffs where the sea breaks in an ever-evocative symphony, never out of harmony with the imagination. Of course, to all this one would have to add the sleepy murmur of the multiplication table, the screech of chalk on the blackboard, the weekly homework, the unframed glasses of the Latin teacher, the sound of new shoes, the ash of papa's cigar . . . . And those beaches are also haunted by undefined blue silhouettes, which maybe represent fear of the dark, and a moving thread of multicolored insects . . .

But what does not exist there, certainly, is an absolute understanding of good and evil. There is no such thing as good and bad children; there are children and nothing more.[1]

The notion that she lived in a special world as a child is reinforced by her writings as a whole, wherein the child's world is presented as something distinct, separate, strange, and incomprehensible for the adult mind. In "Sobre el niño, estos días" ("On the Child, at this Time of Year"), one of the essays in *A la mitad del camino (Halfway Down the Road)*, Matute expresses the idea that a child is essentially solitary, isolated by the limits of his understanding, the strangeness of his world, and the impossibility of communicating. She declares that a child "is something other than a man or woman not yet grown. It is as though he had a different body, not simply a smaller one." The inner world of the child has little or no resemblance to that of the adult he will one day become, and childhood is so much a separate age that "upon leaving it, one is reborn, rather than simply continuing." It is evident that only a peculiarly rich—and perhaps indefinitely extended—childhood could produce such sentiments.

III   *The Early Literary Vocation*

Perhaps the necessary inactivity and increased dependence on imagination resulting from her illness combined to stimulate Ana María's literary and artistic inclinations, her precocious vocation as a writer. "In reality," she recalls, "I cannot say precisely when I began to write, because I always wrote. I do remember that when I was five, I would take a piece of paper, fold it in four, fasten it with a clip and write a story. Always, from my most remote recollection, I know that I wanted to be a writer. I could not imagine being anything else."[2] There are still in existence stories, saved by her mother, which the future novelist wrote at the age of five and illustrated herself. Typical of these is "Fantasías" ("Fantasies"), consisting of sixteen pages with colored drawings, which forms part of the collection of original Matute manuscripts in the Boston University library.[3] While obviously much juvenilia was not preserved, it would seem that her literary and artistic bents enjoyed a continued coexistence until well into adolescence, when the future novelist narrowed her focus exclusively to writing.

Among the unpublished early works preserved are stories which definitely foreshadow constants in her later work, constituting the first eivdence of Matute's sustained interest in certain themes: the interest in children, and in children's literature; tales of fantasy; the frequent presence of the orphan and the solitary child; the preoccupation with time. Bearing in mind the social consciousness of her mature works, it could even be asserted that the germ is present in the five-year-old's "Fantasies," in the unfinished little story entitled "La avaricia de un rey," ("The Avarice of a King")—wherein the poor are dying of hunger. However, this probably reflects not nascent social consciousness but the absorption of the moral teachings commonly given to children in Spanish *colegios* (private schools). Such is the suggestion of another little tale of the same period with a similarly exemplary tendency: A little boy is not granted his wish because he is too lazy ("El duende y el niño," ["The Elf and the Boy"]), and so learns not to be slothful.

The summer months which her family spent in the country were important, too, for the developing literary career. The liberty the children enjoyed there, the acquaintance with people who lived differently, impressed and stimulated her. She began then, and continues to write still, of the fascinating life of the mountains. Her grandmother's house is recalled as simple, square, a "shape any child might draw," with symmetrical windows and a long iron balcony running clear across the façade. Behind it were rock walls, a meadow and produce gardens, and beyond, not too distant, a poplar grove and then the river. The village was in a valley, with mountains rising all around, the forest close on every side. The forest and the river recur obsessively in Matute's writing—in the novels, the short stories, and the non-fiction. Mansilla was small, consisting of but a few dozen houses and one main plaza, surrounded by arcaded buildings, with its skeletal iron bandstand in the center. The highest point was the church tower, with ancient stones golden in the light of afternoon, topped by the stork's nest characteristic of Castile. At the edge of the ancient village stood a hill known as *Pico La Horca* (Hangman's Peak), with its legend of a mayor long ago executed for his refusal to continue paying tribute to the count. The area of the supposed gallows held a macabre fascination for the children, and there are several oblique references to it scattered through Matute's work. The feudal past of the area seems to have been still very much alive in the minds of the villagers, who every year reenacted the hanging of the mayor. Close by stands an ancient hermitage, Santa Catalina, reputed to be over a thousand years old. In a very real sense, the life of the villagers has changed but little in that milennium. One essay in *The River* states that for them, only three things in life really matter—birth, marriage, and death—and consequently, there are for them only three transcendent events: baptisms, weddings, and funerals.

Ana María's illness at the age of eight was particularly significant, for she was sent to live with her grandparents during an extended convalescence, thereby becoming acquainted with a countryside different from that of her summers, with new aspects of life, unknown in her sheltered city existence. "I entered a world that I have never forgotten. The country people of Castile, their problems, their atrocious struggle for life, were revealed to me for the first time."[4] The children of the poor went to work in the fields, as errand boys, or as shepherds, at the age of eight, and only attended school when they did not have something more lucrative to do. The pathetic figure of the child robbed of childhood, prematurely aged by poverty or emotional circumstances, so frequent in Matute's writing, undoubtedly took form with her observations during this period. She wanted to go to the public school in the village (although in Spain, public schools were extremely poor, often located in miserable quarters, and attended only by children of the lowest economic level), and succeeded in being allowed to study with the village children. This experience is recalled, albeit somewhat literarily transformed, in "Los niños buenos" ("The Good Children").

Ana María lived very much in a world of her own, with her puppet theater, her black cloth doll, and especially the river and the forest. No single child seems to have influenced her decisively, although she has recorded several emotionally significant experiences. But if friendships were not decisively important, her observations were. The country people she met then made a deep and lasting impression on her: the women who went to plow with their infants tied to their backs, or left

their newborn children on a blanket, under an umbrella, with their
lunch and water; the fatherless boys who sold their only horse to buy
seeds and pulled the plow themsleves; the schoolmaster who taught
with one of his children in his arms, and wandered through the village
explaining to anyone who would listen the causes of the rain and wind
and redness of the moon. Disquieted by many of these things, she was
affected most of all by the bitterness of the village schoolmasters who
would arrive with high ideals but slowly become brutalized by the
poverty, and scorn, or disdain of the ignorant, ending up drunken,
dirty, with all illusion gone. "It was a very sad thing, then," she notes,
"to be a teacher in the villages of a country that invented the proverbial
comparison of being 'hungrier than a schoolteacher.' "[5] These
characters—villagers, schoolmasters, peasants, doctor, shepherds—
reappear in *Los Abel, Fiesta al noroeste (Celebration in the Northwest)*,
*Los hijos muertos (The Dead Children), Historias de la Artámila (Tales
of Artámila)*, and several other stories.

The novelist's enduring attachment to this piece of rural Castile is
shown also by its frequent appearance as a setting for her works: not
only does it figure as the background of the works just mentioned, but
it also furnishes the environment for *Los niños tontos (The Foolish
Children)* and many of the stories in *El tiempo (Time)* and *El
arrepentido (The Repentant One)*. Today, the beloved landscape of
Matute's childhood, together with the village and her grandmother's
house, have disappeared beneath the waters of a reservoir whose
construction is related in *The Dead Children*. The entire village and its
surroundings were submerged when a high irrigation and power dam
was completed a short distance down the river, not long after the war.
A new, compact village was constructed on higher land overlooking the
lake, and a power plant installed, complete with handsome new houses
for its technical personnel. One or two of Matute's essays refer to
"their" new house, indicating that some family lands remain there and
continue to offer an escape from the busier world of the city, but
nevertheless, the ancient village is irrevocably lost. Many of the former
inhabitants have moved away, and the new village has a provisional air
about it, artificial and sterile. The novelist's lasting sense of loss is
described in several sketches in *The River*, notably the first and fourth,
and one particularly poignant prose poem entitled "El camino" ("The
Road") which appears both in *The River* and in *A la mitad del camino
(Halfway Down the Road)*. The change seems for her evidence of the
inexorable passage of time, her constant preoccupation, and in the face
of it, she prefers to return to the past which is sensed so near, beneath

the waters, somehow identified with the river which continues to flow below the surface of the lake.

The reservoir was constructed by forced labor, by the inmates of a penal colony who lived on the outskirts of the village in conditions of extreme poverty, many with wives and children who had followed them there to live in miserable shacks near the prison. Matute has written of these people in *The Dead Children*, in her censored novel, *Las luciérnagas (The Fireflies)*, and in part of *Halfway Down the Road*. The women, with their resignation, their impassivity contrasting with frequent irrational outbursts, affected her deeply. She found them totally alien, incomprehensible, and despite her obvious sympathy, refers repeatedly to their strangeness. There is no doubt, of course, that they are victims, and even as a child, Matute was perplexed by the inhumanity with which some human beings treated others. A gulf of animosity existed between the village and the penal colony, reflected in the children of the two groups, which led to frequent skirmishes and rock-throwing incidents. One such encounter, witnessed by Ana María at the age of eight or nine, perhaps earlier, she recalls as having profoundly influenced her way of thinking and her vocation as a writer. "I have considered it, and I believe that is what impelled me to write. In other words, that day was born a feeling of impotence against the injustice in the world. It is impossible to explain in words what I wanted to express; I wanted to express disconformity, and I began to write of that." [6]

The incident in question is beautifully retold in "Los chicos" ("The Boys"), part of *Tales of Artamila*. The Matute children had been forbidden to have any contact with the boys from the penal colony. Efren, oldest son of the foreman of the estate, large for his thirteen years and something of a bully, ridiculed their cowardice, and to prove there was nothing to fear from the convicts' children, caught one much smaller boy and beat him brutally. The child took the beating in stoic silence, bleeding and battered, but without crying. Ana María watched, glued to the spot: "I wanted to cry without knowing exactly why. I was only able to repeat to myself: He was just a child. Nothing more than a child, like any other." [7] The novelist has several times mentioned the importance of this incident for her career as a writer, and stated that, next to the Civil War, it influenced her more than any single experience. "That scene, that defenseless back, have never been erased from my mind, and return to me ever and again, as a symbol. Where was good, where was justice?" [8] Matute's frequent treatment of the theme of the cruelty of children (sometimes deliberate, sometimes unconscious, spontaneous) may also spring in part from this experience, as well as her preoccupation with injustice.

Except for the time in the village school when she was eight, Ana María until the age of ten studied alternately in Madrid and Barcelona in *colegios* run by French nuns, an experience which seems to have been mostly unpleasant. She has confessed that the *colegio* was torture for her, and that she went most unwillingly. Education for Spanish girls in those years consisted largely of an exaggerated emphasis on morality, an atmosphere of repression and—as the novelist remembers it—of hypocrisy, false pride, and fear. Her recollection is that everything possible was done to make education unpleasant, and both she and her older sister suffered nightmares because of experiences in the *colegio*, where innocent transgressions were met with threats of divine reprisal in this world and the next. She remembers the nuns as "sinister," and some of her subjective reaction is conveyed by her metaphor describing them as "a rosary of black ants." In one of the essays of *Halfway Down the Road* she mentions a lifelong aversion to ants, which may account for the choice of words. A probable reflection of her feelings for the *colegio* may also be seen in the character of Soledad, protagonist of *The Fireflies* and *En esta tierra (In This Land)*, particularly in the relationship between Soledad and the nuns of her *colegio*, and her feelings of rebelliousness and alienation.

Perhaps because of having glimpsed another world during her stays in the village, Ana María was not content with an existence limited to her home and the *colegio*: she would escape at every opportunity. "It isn't that I was unhappy at home; I wanted to see things that I didn't have at home. I had a great curiosity, an immense curiosity for the world, for people, for everything that occurred around me," she explained. Books in the *colegio* were horrible; there existed few or no good books for children in Spanish literature, only tales of "good guys" and "bad guys" intended to inculcate virtue. She recalled one in particular, entitled "Buena Juanita" ("Good Jane"), in which Juanita (the model to imitate) was a *chivata*, a "squealer" or tattle-tale who denounced her schoolmates. Matute's interest in children's literature may well originate in part as a reaction to her youthful distaste for what then passed as juvenile fiction. Among her unpublished juvenilia, a passage in "El trozo de espejo" ("The Piece of Mirror") suggests her attitude. The story is undated, but the handwriting, spelling, and level of complexity would indicate that it was written at perhaps nine or ten. Two boys whose plans have gone awry are described as "more long-faced and sad, ill-humored and out of sorts than if they had just read a whole book of instructive stories for children."

The days spent in the *colegio* are at least partially responsible for another aspect of Matute's work. Recalling her lack of attentiveness, and how she would gaze at her surroundings or write stories in her workbooks, she mentions the sunlight on the walls of her first classrooms, with their "fascinating prints of Cain and Abel." Her use of the motif, as well as her pity for Cain, seems to have originated early.

Outside the *colegio*, Ana María read things more to her liking: translations of *Alice in Wonderland, Peter Pan*, the stories of Hans Christian Andersen and the brothers Grimm, nearly all of the accessible literature of fantasy. Her "Bible," she declared, was *Alice in Wonderland*. "To it I owe my acceptance of the absurd in life. Reading it, I was in my element. It is not a common style; the absurd is not easy. I think there are very few people who understand it."[9] From much of her juvenilia and occasional references in her adult works, the importance of Hans Christian Andersen is also apparent. "December and Andersen," part of the collection *Halfway Down the Road,* relates that one of the most decisive influences of her childhood was a book of tales by Andersen, which she received as a present from the Three Kings, the Spanish substitute for Santa Claus. Having subsequently lost this much-prized possession, she spent twenty-four years hoping to regain it, and at last a friend presented her with one of the few remaining copies of the same original edition, taken from the publisher's archives. Rereading it as an adult, she found its magic undiminished. Her recollection is that one illustration, "The Gnome and the Storekeeper," was responsible for her first coming to understand the difference between material and spiritual riches. This is a key concept in her writing, both the unpublished juvenilia and the adult works, perhaps the basis of *The Fireflies* and the current trilogy, *Los mercaderes (The Merchants)*, as well as many of her works of fantasy.

The family's periodic shifts between Madrid and Barcelona led to further difficulty in the *colegio*, for Ana María came to have a persistent feeling of being an outsider, always being from somewhere else. In the rivalry and hostility between the two regions she was excluded from both: in Madrid she was called the "Catalana," and in Barcelona, the "Castellana." The constant sensation of solitude in her works, the numerous lonely and misunderstood children, may not result exclusively from these experiences, but it is clear, at least, that the novelist has personal knowledge of them, and that her sense of alienation during these childhood years has had its part in the obsessive recreation of these sentiments.

During the last year of attendance at the religious *colegio* in Madrid, Ana María had a teacher (not a nun, but a lay person) whom she remembers as particularly important in her intellectual development. This lady was unusually liberal—for Spain—in her teaching methods, and introduced the nine-year-old girl to the works of García Lorca. Because of this teacher, María Jesús Castilla, her attitude toward the *colegio* changed briefly. Where before she had always gone dragging her feet and longing to escape, she recalls that during these few months, she went with pleasure and anticipation. She was emphatic, however, that this was the only time. Her early acquaintance with and enthusiasm for the works of Lorca undoubtedly served to strengthen the lyrical vein in Matute, another constant in her work. While there is insufficient cause to speak of influence, Lorca appears to have been the only Spanish author whom she enjoyed as a child, and this, too, is significant.

Ana María's literary vocation was constant as well as precocious, and throughout her childhood she wrote: stories for and about children, stories of fantasy, of imaginary worlds, of animals, warriors and princesses, gnomes and dwarfs, often stimulated by her readings of history, legends, and stories, inside the *colegio* and out. She continued to paint and draw, with children's heads the favorite subject.[10] Considering the novelist's lasting interest in children and adolescents (who overshadow and outnumber her adult characters), this youthful predilection for children even as subjects for painting or drawing subjects is not an insignificant detail. Then, too, there is a point of coincidence between many of these drawings and her literary characterizations which is particularly striking. In both, a special importance is given the eyes, which are unusually large in the drawings—often disproportionately so—and which tend to be the primary or most revealing feature in fictional presentations.

Of delicate health, with prolonged illnesses, but by no means an invalid; introspective, given to fantasy, with a special sensitivity to nature and the world around her; precocious in her literary vocation and her social consciousness, but apparently not considered unusual as a child, Ana María was not really deeply wounded by life before the summer of 1936.

CHAPTER 2

The Civil War and the Writer

I The Subjective Impact of the War

THE OUTBREAK of the Spanish Civil War in July, 1936, a few days before Matute's tenth birthday, changed the world she had known until then. "Obviously, the Spanish war was a decisive impact on my life. I was only ten—or perhaps for that very reason—but those three years, first of revolution and afterward of war, marked me deeply. The discovery that there was 'another city' and 'other people' that I had not even suspected, with hates and desires that had never been revealed to me, was tremendous. I remember the burnings, the violence, those bodies that would appear at dawn in the outlying fields. It was all so terribly new for me, that up to that moment I lived, you might say, in a crystal urn."[1]

The Matute family was in Barcelona when the conflict began, in the Republican zone, and there they remained for the duration, as travel within Spain became impossible. One immediate consequence of the civil strife was the closing of the religious schools, and as a result Ana María and other children of her family studied with private professors. Some of these were priests who had gone into hiding upon the closing of the religious institutions; one of them has left a probable literary counterpart in Ramón Boloix, the private professor of Soledad and her brother in *En esta tierra (In This Land)*. The Matute family was fortunate enough to lose no close relatives during the war, although one or more of Ana María's professors were killed in the attempt to escape to France during the closing months of the conflict.

The importance of the Civil War for the future novelist cannot be too strongly emphasized; she herself has repeatedly mentioned its significance. For Matute, as for nearly all writers of her generation, "The Civil War was a decisive wound which marked forever my life as a writer."[2] It spelled the end of childhood, of security, and shook the foundations of her world and of her views about it, leaving an indelible imprint on memories, beliefs, and preoccupations. Many contemporary Spanish writers consider the Civil War the most significant experience of their lives, regardless of the part of Spain in which they might have spent the years of hostilities, but the war's impact was particularly strong in Barcelona, with its large concentration of anarchists and radical leftists among the industrial workers. Here civil and social unrest was at a height, and during the initial months, the population knew the horrors not only of civil war, but of a bloody social revolution. Although Matute does not distinguish between the two, various elements in her recollections seem to indicate that those things which most disturbed and perplexed her were social in nature.

As Barcelona was a prime area of anarcho—syndicalist activity and of other leftist labor movements, much class hostility, class vengeance, and terrorism centered there, both prior to the war and after its outbreak, increasing in tempo after the rebellion of General Franco, when the Republican government distributed arms to the populace. In Barcelona, Workers' Committees armed and organized militia, and simultaneously carried on the war against the insurgents while stepping up action against suspected Fascists in their midst. "Public safety committees," formed by representatives of the three working-class parties, selected the victims, and the executions were carried out by small groups of men who took them from their homes in the dead of night for *paseos* (rides). In addition, there were mass executions of Fascist suspects taken by mobs from the prisons, either in reprisal for air raids, or for reported Fascist atrocities. This was replaced by a police terror, under mounting Communist control, exerted both against dissident leftists and suspected Fascists.

On the side of the Nationalist insurgents, there was also terror, at least in part deliberately instigated for the intimidation of their enemies, to do away with troublesome opponents. Falangist and Carlist militia appeared, with previously prepared lists of victims, and executions took place on an unprecedented scale. In many towns, everyone associated with the Republic (including even postal workers, school-masters, and other minor functionaries whose jobs did not indicate political affiliations) died before the firing squads. The method of execution was similar, with the victims taken from their homes in the pre-dawn hours and shot outside the towns. And in the Fascist prisons, executions without trial were a daily occurrence, until these institutions had been filled and emptied many times.

At the onset of the war in July, the Matute family was preparing to leave for Mansilla de la Sierra to spend their summer vacation. The conflict immediately split Spain into two distinctly separate zones, with Barcelona in the Republican or Loyalist zone, and Mansilla in the area controlled by the insurgents. Thus, in addition to the horrors of war, Ana María suffered because of the enforced separation from her beloved countryside. Her father's factory in Barcelona was collectivized, as were many others, in a series of events profoundly perplexing and disturbing for the young writer, thereby constrained to reevaluate her concept of private property and a host of other basic notions. While her family did not actually suffer from hunger, much of the war was experienced directly, and Ana María was witness to bombings, violence, terror, and death.

In part, no doubt, as an escape from these things, but also to fill the hours no longer occupied by the *colegio*, Ana María during the war years "founded" a juvenile magazine, *La Revista de Shybil* (*Shybil's Review*), for her brothers, sisters, and cousins. She wrote all the contents, and as was her practice with her stories, illustrated the magazine herself. She was also, in her words, editor, director, typographer, publisher, and distributor—but it must be noted that most issues consisted of a single copy. *Shybil's Review* was not exempt from war-time rationing, and used a coarse, brown paper, probably also limited in quantity. An examination of the contents of this little magazine yields a goodly number of insights into the interests and activities of its author and readers. There are columns on movie stars of particular appeal among the younger public, jokes, recipes, suggested tricks to play on friends, "letters to the editor," designs for dresses, the serialized life of "Shybil" and a rather broad and varied selection of original stories written by Ana María. Many of these are incomplete, the promised continuations either having disappeared or never having materialized. There are quite a few laudatory advertisments for "A.M.M.," and for her books and stories, announcements of translations of her novels, and exhortations to read forthcoming issues, all of which might be mere childish wishful thinking, but which possibly evinces the tenacity of Matute's early literary aspirations.

Looking back to the war years, the mature novelist observed: "You cannot imagine how much I enjoyed writing that magazine, the great refuge that it was for me in those days. We lived shut in, fearful, barely in contact with other children, and in that magazine I was able to express myself and say many things I would never have dared to say aloud—something of the reflection of things I saw, and always *clamoring romantically* for justice. All of that, naturally, makes one smile now." [3] The number of titles of stories announced in *Shybil's*

Review (including even a trilogy) suggests that perhaps much juvenilia has been lost, or not yet made available to public view, and such material may correspond more closely to the novelist's recollection. But the preserved issues of the little magazine do not contain too many instances of "clamoring for justice," a theme of great importance later. Rather, there is evidence of a very natural desire to escape the unpleasant and upsetting environment of Civil War Spain, with a good deal of temporal and spatial exoticism. This aspect is worth noting because it is not a constant in Matute, all but disappearing from her writings a few years later.

Many constants, however, do appear in the stories—most of them written at ten, eleven, and twelve years of age—in *Shybil's Review*. The consistent emphasis in description is on eyes, hands, and hair, with repeated observations that eyes were the most "characteristic" feature. Already the use of the orphan as a character is frequent (although it should be noted, for those unfamiliar with the Spanish usage, that the child who has lost only one parent is also called an orphan). The incidence of orphans and of parent mortality is consistently high in all periods of Matute's writing. Accompanying this are the themes of solitude and loneliness; the solitary child, often sick, is a frequent figure, as is the "different" child, set apart either by deformities, special sensibilities, or an unusual imagination. These creations in her early work often anticipate, or embody the same traits later found in various of the portraits in *Los niños tontos (The Stupid Children)*.

There is considerable sentimentalism in the early stories, although usually handled with taste and restraint. Occasional reminders of folk tales and an echo of Andersen's "The Poor Little Match Girl" can be heard, with the orphan child barefoot in the snow on Christmas Eve, typical of the physical and emotional atmosphere of many of the novelist's youthful creations. She tends to use paired opposites such as, for example, the selfish rich child and the unselfish little waif, or the tall, strong, dark brother, and the slender, delicate, blond brother. Contrasting physical characteristics almost always go hand-in-hand with opposite subjective traits. At times this is not accomplished with too much subtlety but nevertheless, considering the age of the writer, her intuitive awareness of the possible effects to be achieved through the manipulation of contrasts evinces an instinct for the dramatic beyond her years.

A particularly striking aspect is the novelist's early concern with happiness, on an abstract or philosophical plane. Happiness figures as either the major theme or topic for reflection in several of the juvenile compositions. Even in pre-adolescence she seems to have concluded that happiness is not easy, or lasting; that the gift of happiness is part of the patrimony of magicians and fairy godmothers, but not the world of reality; and that moments of happiness are brief, and possibly not appreciated at the time.[4]

Just exactly how much of this is a result of the Civil War is probably impossible to calculate, but there can be no doubt that the things she witnessed and experienced then played an important part. Since the pessimism of her later works has been a subject of study,[5] its probable origins are of interest. Combined with her tendency to idealize childhood, to separate it totally from the world of the adult, there would seem to be an unconscious identification of childhood and happiness, with the conviction that one must end as inevitably as the other. This is not unique with Matute, since many Spanish writers of her generation (notably, for example, Juan Goytisolo) view childhood at times as something of a "paradise lost," again suggesting that the role of the Civil War was crucial in the formation of this attitude. The phenomenon seems of sufficient significance to merit further consideration of the novelist's comments on it.

Children of the middle class in pre-Civil War Spain led an exceedingly sheltered existence, between religious boarding schools, their homes, and the family's intimates. They were so isolated and shut off from the world that Ana María was able to refer to her first ten years as life "in a crystal urn," or "wrapped in cotton." Suddenly, shockingly, the Civil War changed all this:

With that ambiguous feeling between surprise and rebellion which all children experience before actions they consider unjust, we were violently shown the other side of that world in which we had been so utterly submerged. Suddenly we were shown, with all its crudeness, that "atrocious" world, that world which had been damned for us in advance. Overnight, we children had to ask ourselves why the nuns from our school were wearing street clothes, why they fled or hid; why our father's factory was no longer our father's; why had the good, clean, upright, honest, pleasing-to-the-sight-of-the-Lord world raised so much hatred? Who, if these were officially the good people, actually were the bad people? A handful of bewildered children, kneeling on the balconies, from behind half-closed shutters, observed the armed men, men they had never seen before, running through the streets: dark, unfortunate men with faces of fear and hate, with red handkerchiefs around their necks, were pointing rifles and machine guns at the "decent" houses.[6]

The reaction to this new world, first of incomprehension and perplexity, later of attempts to understand, included a profound sensation of injustice, a loss of many prior beliefs, a complete reorganization of values. "I understood that those acts of violence were due to some motive, and that motive had never been explained to me. Nothing is gratuitous in this world, and a child of ten intuits these things clearly."[7]

Around what we had considered to be immutably good or evil appeared a cloud of doubt. Who now could define the right hand or the left hand of God? Who could point this out decisively, on what map, in what country, in what paradise? Where was goodness, justice? A thousand questions assaulted the world we had considered secure, sensible, unquestionable . . . men, women, and children, surrounding a microphone, clamored, challenged, triumphed over a word, a word new to us: *liberty*.

A group of bewildered children observed; we were anxious, curious, expectant. A child of ten is struck by these things and asks that incessant and obsessive question with the cutting simplicity of childhood: *Why?* And life—torn to pieces, violent, till then unknown, but certainly palpitating life—opened up before our eyes. The world was hunger. The world was hate. It was also the desire for justice; and it was egotism, fear, horror, cruelty and death.[8]

These were the circumstances which formed the attitudes of Ana María Matute and her generation of writers. Those who experienced the Civil War as children "lost their paradise" overnight, and with it, innocence, credulity, security. Never again could they be satisfied with pat explanations or accept tranquilly a privileged position in the old order of things, the world for which they had been prepared. Forced to think for themselves, they grew into doubting, questioning, nonconforming adolescents and adults, expressing their revolt and opposition in their writings and looking obsessively backward to that moment when their childhood abruptly ended. This, at least in part, is the origin of the preoccupation with the child and adolescent which characterizes a great many postwar Spanish novelists, and most particularly Matute.

Two relatively long compositions, both dated 1938, "Alegoría" ("Allegory") and "Volflorindo," are of particular interest as anticipations of the novelist's works of fantasy written in her maturity. They already illustrate her basic dualism, whereby mankind is divided into dreamers and utilitarians (characteristic of some of her realistic writings as well). This division is central to at least two major works, the censored novel, *The Fireflies*, and the trilogy, *The Merchants*. In these childhood fantasies, the dreamers and idealists, of necessity solitary, are not understood by those lacking their vision, and are even considered crazy by the more practical, who have either lost their illusions and idealism, or never had them. The related theme of the importance of "beautiful" lies, fantasy or daydreaming and other forms of illusion is also found in these surviving bits of Matute's juvenilia. Many of the adventures of Volflorindo, the protagonist of the story of that name, owe a debt to Hans Christian Andersen, both in structure and theme: his visit to the Land of the Multiplication Table is probably an antecedent of the children's book published by the mature novelist as *El país de la pizarra (Blackboard Land)*; and at least two other episodes suggest the inspiration of *Alice in Wonderland*. Even as a child, however, Matute was not a mere imitator: most of the creatures are original, and Volflorindo's humor is peculiarly his own. Many jokes concern his disproportionately large head, a rather cruel sort of humor at the expense of something not essentially funny. This rather uncommon humor does not reappear elsewhere in Matute's writing, although she does write of deformed children on a number of occasions. While others may ridicule them through cruelty or insensitivity, the novelist's own mood is compassionately lyric and tender. Like others in Matute's later works, Volflorindo looks backward wistfully until he returns at last to the scenes of his childhood, his imaginary world, and recovers his childlike joys. This theme, with refinements and variations, is so frequent that it is of particular interest to find it so early in this writer's work. It is not rare for the adult to idealize childhood, looking backward nostalgically, but it is somewhat unusual to find the same idea treated, and almost obsessively, by a twelve-year-old. The realization that the war had definitely ended an epoch, and the sense of loss underlying her many treatments of this theme, seem to have come early to Matute.

Her other major source of amusement or distraction during the war was a marionette theater, in connection with which she invented comedies for her brothers and sisters. The marionette theater, like the Castilian countryside and the Civil War, is a recurrent theme in her mature works, although slightly less obsessive and probably less significant. It is no coincidence that Matute's first full-length novel, *Pequeño teatro (Little Theater),* is a complex symbol based on the analogy between theater and life, reality and farce, human beings and puppets. This theme or leitmotiv also appears in *Fiesta al noroeste (Celebration in the Northwest)* and in *Primera memoria (First Memoirs)* and more briefly in other works.

II   *Adolescence and Further Juvenilia*

The Civil War ended at last with the triumph of the insurgent forces, and their revolt began to be called "The Glorious Uprising." Intolerant, totalitarian, vindictive, the new regime brought a new period of trial for Spain. The war's end did not signal an end to bloodshed and terror; there was added the atmosphere of the police state; and Spain, with industries ruined and crops destroyed, faced problems of massive reconstruction, widespread shortages, hunger, and unemployment. The housing problem was acute, the cost of living exorbitant, and the bare necessities of existence became objects of black-market speculation and profiteering. And at the same time, censorship and repression combined with unending persecution of the political enemies of the regime. "After the experience of war we were able to understand the great lesson of words not uttered, of bitten-off cries, and the great dull silence of the increasingly oppressive gag over thousands of mouths, ears, eyes, and finally, over thoughts,"[9] wrote Matute years later. Repeating the words of another novelist of her generation, she called these things the "horrors of peace."

With the war's end, Ana María returned to a *colegio*, no longer a religious one, for she and her older sister begged to be sent to a secular school. She resumed studies leading to the *bachillerato* (the approximate equivalent of a high school diploma), but abandoned this course altogether two years later, in 1941, to devote herself to writing, art, and music. She studied painting and drawing with Nuria Llimona and violin with Juan Massia.

There is an added sophistication in the unpublished juvenile writings of these years, predominantly of the fairy tale or slightly fantastic folk tale variety. Some of the childish errors in spelling characteristic of the earlier period have disappeared, and narrative self-consciousness and complexity have increased. One of the most striking advances is in style: this seems to have been the time at which the future novelist became aware of the importance not only of what, but also of how she narrated. There is an intense new lyricism, tenderness, and sensitivity, together with a renewed awareness of beauty. Her vocabulary is noticeably expanded, and her syntax becomes less straightforward, more complicated. The conversational or colloquial tone occasionally employed earlier seems to have all but disappeared, along with an infrequent wry, understated humor. The characteristic rhetorical figure of earlier works, the simile, is joined by the metaphor, employed timidly at first and then more confidently. At the same time, her never absent idealism becomes more marked.

In "El hijo de la luna" ("The Son of the Moon"), written in 1940, the preoccupation with happiness again appears, in the familiar atmosphere of fantasy. A hideous gnome, Logo, so grotesque that he keeps himself hidden from view, nonetheless worships beauty, and is rapturously enamored of the cold perfection of the Moon. Sometimes he sadly sings a song, whose untranslatable refrain, "luna, lunera" [10] is repeated by a group of moon-mad children. In this artfully constructed work, wherein repetition is employed as an effective lyric technique, the idea is developed that real beauty must be warm and emotional. Beauty, truth, happiness, and love all seem to blend into one, identified with the warm and loving home—which the forest children have abandoned for an illusion, not valuing their happiness because it was humble and lacking in exterior beauty. Logo, having seen the beauty of the loving home, persuades the Son of the Moon to risk his own destiny and return the children to their parents, to return to dreaming instead of trying to live a dream.

There are numerous parallels again with Anderson; the figure of the Moon strongly recalls the Snow Queen, and the basic theme is identical: that of a young mind blinded for a time to the "true values" of love, faith, home, and humble beauty by the cold, abstract beauty of the Moon, the Snow Queen, or exaggerations of the intellect (symbolized by mathematics in Anderson's tale, and by art—song and dance—in Matute's). There are at least two indications elsewhere in Matute's writing of the significance of this particular tale: the use of the name, Kai, in *Cumbres* (*Summits*), and repeated references to Kay and Gerda, the little protagonists of "The Snow Queen," by Matia in *First Memoirs*. Several elements evoke the folk tale, especially the theme frequent in much early literature of the moon bewitching or stealing children. The open book is used as a concrete symbol of the importance of dreams in the life of the child, the positive "warm" type of dream. The conclusion reached with regard to happiness seems to be that it lies in the ability to appreciate what one has, or at least in the proper esteem for those things the average person has: home, family, love, books, dreams.

"Lucecitas de plata" ("The Little Silver Lights"), also dated 1940, is the only Matute work to combine fantasy and a fair dosage of religious elements. In some respects similar to the "Allegory" discussed previously, it is relatively more sophisticated, and seems a direct antecedent of one of the stories of *Tres y un sueño (Three [Fantasies] and a Dream)*, published some twenty years later. A poor orphan, overworked and mistreated but happy because he lives in his fantasies, converses with nature, seeing the invisible creatures of fancy, is taken by gnomes to visit their world in order that he never forget them, even when grown to manhood (since they depend on having humans believe in them). Afterward, Tilín, the boy with the "little silver lights" in his eyes which had allowed him to see the gnomes, is so unhappy because he cannot return to their marvelous world that be becomes dangerously ill. (The later story could, with slight variations, use the same summary up to this point; subsequently there is a divergence.) Tilín realizes too late that his happiness was more real than that of the gnomes, since he possesses an immortal soul, the thing they desire most. But he is already dying, and only has time to will the silver lights to the old man who had formerly exploited and abused him. At this juncture, the author brings fantasy and religion together, employing the ideas of forgiveness, repentance, and redemption. The "little silver lights" enable the old man to see not only the gnome who brings them, but his former self, and to realize the wrong he has done. He goes to church, where he seems to see Tilín stretching out his arms from above, and is found dead on his knees at the close of the service. Illusion, dreams, idealism, the work implies, are also a part of salvation.

Consideration of these works in conjunction with the situation and events in Spain at the time of their composition shows the relation to be largely a negative one, with the future novelist taking refuge in a realm of fantasy and idealism quite in contrast with exterior reality. Nevertheless, she was shortly to turn to writing with a more realistic setting and content, characterizing not only her first publications, but the bulk of her production for the next fifteen years. *Cumbres (Summits)* the only work in dramatic form written by Matute to date, is in several ways a transition from the somewhat stylized, ideal plane of conception of the preceding compositions to the plane of contemporary and concretely localized realism where succeeding works would be situated. Although *Summits* is undated, its transitional nature as well as its level of complexity and sophistication dictate placing it within the period limited at one extreme by the juvenilia just considered and at the other by her first published novel, *Los Abel (The Abel Family)*. The baroque nature of *Summits*, with its various levels of symbolism, immediately brings to mind *Pequeño teatro (Little Theater)*, since both works share a partly fantastic, partly realistic outlook and narrative point of view, and both are loaded with symbols and idealism. This suggests composition at approximately the same period, quite possible since *Little Theater*, although not published until 1954, was written some eleven years earlier. Following this line of reasoning, *Summits* should have been written about 1942. While its philosophical implications, and even perhaps some of the practical ones, are at times more profound than those of *Little Theater*, its artistic conception and development are immeasurably less subtle, so that in terms of craftsmanship, *Summits* must be considered an earlier work, or else it becomes necessary to explain how the novelist happened to take a giant step backward.

Despite her early enthusiasm for her marionette theater and the frequent appearance of this motif in her narratives, Matute has made only this one unpublished attempt at play writing. The result of her effort she herself described laughingly as *muy mala* ("very bad"), and the truth is that while on an intellectual level much of *Summits* is admirable, it is not appropriate for dramatic representation. The problems and conflicts involved are too intellectualized, stated on much too abstract a level, so that what the work gains in philosophical or ethical substance, it loses in theatrical potential. Another disadvantage, from the dramatic point of view, is that it depends relatively little on the action and dialogue, and too much on evocation (of a distant, invisible setting), and on the public's apprehension of the symbols. Most important of all, the central situation or problem—the division of men into idealists and materialists—does not of itself produce a dramatic conflict, although if sufficiently removed from the abstract, it has the potential to do so.

The "summits" represent not only the mountain heights, but some type of ideal purity as well, accessible only to those who renounce the material comforts of the valley and live close to nature and far from the world. There is some ambiguity as to whether these are the heights of faith, or of moral and ethical integrity, or selfless devotion to an ideal, or something of all of these. The spell of the peaks is such that no one who has ever reached them, ever lived there, can be content elsewhere—living near them is something which means more than love, even than a great love, but at the same time, it is not possible for everyone. To some it is given only to look upward, and others are content to live in the valley without even a glimpse of the summits. *No todos somos iguales* is repeated several times: "we are not all alike."

There are intensely lyric moments, of poetic fantasy such as the description of the shepherd whose eyes are blue from so much looking at the sky, or the lyric tenderness in the tale of the almond tree loved by generations, evolving through successive carvings at last into a slim wooden ring signifying the promise of love. The setting, "the North," is vaguely Scandinavian or Swiss, but the emotions, the problems, even the symbols are universal. This use of mountains and a northern setting seems to be a combination of the novelist's love for the mountains of her childhood summers and another unconscious echo of Hans Christian Andersen, who locates most of his tales in the north. The most immediate and pertinent antecedent among Spaniards in the use of the cardinal symbols of mountain, valley, and lake, is Miguel de Unamuno in his novelette, *San Manuel Bueno, mártir*. In both, the mountain at times takes on the meaning of faith, illusion, dreams, aspirations, the constant reminder of a goal, and happiness. The symbolism of the valleys does not coincide to the same extent; for Unamuno the valley signified deprivation, anguish, encircling death, while Matute equates it largely with material and egotistical preoccupations.

Matute's interest in happiness is evident again in *Summits*, and while its existence is debated, and denied by at least one character, the author's own position seems to have evolved to the point of considering happiness largely a function of memory: "Happiness exists, but it is short; it passes quickly, and therefore where it truly resides is in memories, not in the moment."[11] This conclusion, applied to the basic idealist-materialist dualism leads to the discovery that dreamers and idealists are able to be happy with the memory of a moment, while the more materialistic need to live such moments continually. "Life," according to one of those from the summits, "is condensed in a few moments, a few hours, perhaps a year. The rest of existence is empty, bitter, hard. Therefore, if we know how to live those moments intensely, then, drawing away from everything else, we become saturated with the memory ... That is how to find the small happiness allowed us on Earth."[12] A correlative of the dualism, and another constant in Matute is the incompatibility of material success and idealism. Any large degree of material success seems fatally denied the dreamer, because of his nature or his scruples. And a parallel, a second correlative would be that the materially successful consider the idealist a crazy, romantic dreamer, unrealistic and at odds with life.

In 1942, when Ana Maria Matute was sixteen, "El chico de al lado" ("The Boy Next Door"),[13] a short story and her first published work, appeared in the Barcelona magazine, *Destino*. The following year, 1943, she interrupted her studies of painting and music to devote herself exclusively to literature. *Little Theater*, completed this same year, remained unpublished due to a series of chance factors until 1954, when it appeared in a slightly revised version:

These were difficult times for Spanish writers. The novel, subject to stringent moral, political and religious censorship, could only support virtue, the regime and the church; it could reflect nothing but a spurious hero or the definitive triumph of decency over indecency, of the angels over the demons; the "good guys" and the "bad guys" once again, as in the tales of our childhood.[14]

The censorship of all publications, mass media, entertainments, and more or less public behavior, as well as the attitudes supporting such repressive control, affected not only the aspiring writers but the climate of daily life in the nation at large. Because most foreign books were prohibited and even the Spanish classics expurgated, there began a traffic in contraband books which was to last for many years. Until well into the sixties, bookstores had their *infernillo* (little hell) where "condemned" books were sold, at abnormally high prices. Spanish authors, in order to publish, were forced to exercise a self-censorship, or to disguise their messages behind symbols, allegories, and other tricks to mislead the censors. The average citizen, skeptical of the controlled press, gave up reading, and because speaking out and acting frankly were dangerous, the normal human tendency to hypocrisy was greatly increased:

Those of us who were then eighteen or twenty began to write in this suffocating environment. It was difficult. For five or ten years we were the rebellious children whom time would defeat and who were to be treated with a heavy hand. We struggled, but our worst enemy was not the open criticism, nor even the censor. It was the surrounding stupor, it was the indifference and disdain for anything literary or intellectual. No one read. No one was interested in literature . . . . But we wanted to write, not for escape or for pleasure, but to denounce.

The censor dismembered our books.

. . . . Between aseptic indifference and bought critics who labeled as Existentialist all they did not understand or approve, we turned our eyes back to the war. And this is easily explained since we had watched it with ignorant, open eyes as it penetrated us; it finally became a way of seeing, vision itself. But the brilliance of what was revealed hurt us, and we were cut off from it, suddenly and brutally. We were surrounded only by echoes, distant rumblings. The words "liberty" and "the rights of man" were torn from our writings and erased from our program. And social justice, that justice for which we were clamoring, they changed to the word "charity."[15]

It was in this atmosphere, and in reaction to it, that *Little Theater* was written, when Matute was seventeen. "Perhaps because it is in adolescence that we are most wounded by hypocrisy and falseness, this novel, where reality and lies are mixed almost without transition, was written, I remember, with great sadness. Writing that book, mixing reality and farce, feeling hate for lies and love for dreams, and at the same time a great nostalgia, I think I lived a little, once again, that childhood time when I invented comedies in my puppet theater. The strongest impulse which dominated me in this book was, perhaps, to denounce that false 'charity'. . ." [16] It was taboo in the novels written immediately after the war for any character to commit suicide or adultery, and the fact that the protagonist of *Little Theater* drowns herself at the end may help to explain why the novel remained unpublished for eleven years.

After leaving the *colegio*, Matute continued her studies on her own, reading more than before, reading everything, but especially novels, essays, and criticism. She discovered forbidden books in the backs of certain bookstores, and so became acquainted with new names and new literary tendencies. She met other young intellectuals interested in literature, restless and rebellious like herself, and began to see them frequently. Of the many aspiring writers in this little group, not all have devoted themselves seriously to literature, but some have subsequently become well known, including Juan Goytisolo, Carlos Barral, and Lorenzo Gomis. They held periodic literary discussions, their own seminar, and despite the official frustrations and restrictions, Matute recalls this period with considerable pleasure. Her friends were lively, interesting, stimulating, and her family's position and indulgence allowed her to live her youth very much as she pleased, even when it included, as she said, "reacting a little against the current, against the family environment." [17]

Among these other incipient writers, all young, idealistic, and somewhat nonconformist, she felt that she had found her way of life and the people with whom she wanted to live. They wrote; they met and read and discussed each other's works. They criticized, praised, suggested improvements, mutually influencing each other for better or for worse. This pattern of life, occasionally underscored by the date of a publication, was to continue essentially uninterrupted for the next several years, until the time of Matute's marriage. To judge on the basis of her repeated declarations in interviews, as well as the reflection of her experiences in her work, the basic ingredients were now complete. The crucial periods for her future writing are her own childhood and adolescence, an importance reflected by the attention she devotes to these periods in the lives of the characters she creates. The novelist's experiences beyond this point do not seem to have contributed significantly to shaping her outlook or in forming her thematics, and from this point onward she offers very little information on her personal life.

CHAPTER 3

The Budding Novelist

LOS ABEL (The Abel Family), which Ana María Matute wrote in 1954, was destined to be the first of her novels to appear in print—the first, and in her own judgment, probably the worst. In later years, she confessed shame of this early effort: "I was nineteen when I wrote it, and the bad thing about that is, it shows:"[1] The novelist's verdict is probably sound; the novel is, in fact, inferior to the greater part of her other work. Despite this, and a certain ineptness notwithstanding, it is a respectable first novel, and important insofar as it represents a tremendous advance in the direction of reality. It is likewise of particular significance for the introduction of the Cain and Abel theme, repeated thereafter almost obsessively, in *Celebration in the Northwest, Three Fantasies and a Dream, The Dead Children* and *First Memoirs*, as well as being implicitly present whenever Matute writes of the Civil War. As the title suggests, *The Abel Family* relates a conflict between brothers, and hence could be considered a symbolic representation of the civil strife. Subsequent treatments of this motif leave no doubt that such is, indeed, its import.

The Abel Family was submitted in 1947 to the competition for the Premio Nadal, a prize established some three years previously for the purpose of discovering promising new novelistic talents at a time when the Spanish literary scene was, to say the least, discouraging. The first Nadal Prize was won by *Nada (Nothing)* of Carmen Laforet, and the unprecedented success of this novel helped to establish the prestige of the prize, while at the same time it created a fairly sure market for subsequent Nadal winners. This prize has continued to exist until the present, and is one of Spain's most coveted and best-known literary awards, despite occasional errors in selection, and some suspicion that economic considerations at times override the purely literary. *The Abel Family* was named a "finalist," or runner-up to *La sombra del ciprés es alargada (Long is the Cypress' Shadow)*, the first novel of Miguel

Delibes. Delibes today is, like Matute, one of Spain's most distinguished narrators, so losing to him (apparently Matute's only loss in literary competition) is no humiliation.

The reasons for mentioning the beginnings of the Nadal Prize are not purely historical, since there is a rather good possibility that the first winner, *Nada*, may have influenced some aspects of *The Abel Family*. *Nada* won the prize at the end of 1944, and the first edition appeared in the spring of 1945, the same year in which Matute wrote *The Abel Family*. *Nada* was immensely popular, and was published in very nearly a literary vacuum, which increases the likelihood of its influencing works written at that time. Then, too, the author of *Nada* was a young girl, only a few years older than Matute herself. These considerations are adduced to suggest one explanation why Ana María Matute wrote *The Abel Family* at the time and in the particular fashion that she did. The differences between this novel and the previous works—both the unpublished juvenilia and *Little Theater*—are so marked that they suggest some cause beyond the continuing evolution away from fantasy, toward realism, already seen beginning in *Summits*. And there are striking parallels in certain basic aspects of the two novels, even though there is enough originality in *The Abel Family* to remove any question of imitation. Both novels portray life within somewhat abnormal families, most or all of whose members represent different psychological aberrations. In both, family life is close to civil warfare on a limited scale, with as much hate as love, and more conflict than harmony in their domestic relationships. Both are narrated by a young girl, a member of the family but emotionally estranged therefrom. In both cases, the narrators are orphans, whose isolation is the greater for their being almost completely friendless, alienated from the rest of the world around them. Each has only one girlfriend, but in neither case is the friendship entirely satisfactory, or one which permits full and frank communication.

So much for the parallels; perhaps more could be found if needed. On the one hand, a work quite different from anything she had written previously, and on the other, coincidences apparently beyond the level of chance indicate a good probability that Matute was inspired by *Nada* in her creation of at least parts of *The Abel Family*. Beyond this, however, her work is very much an independent narrative, with its plot and characters quite clearly differentiated from those of Laforet, and presenting individual variations even within the parallel elements or situations.

The year following participation in the Nadal competition, *The Abel*

Family was published by Destino, the Barcelona firm sponsoring the prize. As a matter of fact, Destino had first contracted to publish *Little Theater* instead, but after the editors read *The Abel Family*, they considered the second novel more mature and changed the contract. The author did not share their judgment, believing *Little Theater* the better of the two, but thus it happened that her first novel was bypassed in favor of the second. Its publication did not go unnoticed; there were interviews in the newspapers, and some two months later, in December, on Radio Barcelona. The criticism, largely if not entirely favorable, was at its worst benign, as Spanish critics tend to judge the novice by quite different standards than those they apply to the mature writer. Despite the young novelist's own lack of satisfaction with the book, she could consider its reception encouraging. Ana María Matute was twenty-one, and her novelistic career was officially launched.

I *The Abel Family*

Plots in Matute's works tend to be somewhat disconnected, vague, and rambling, making brief summary all but impossible. Then, too, the special importance of characterization and of certain obsessive themes makes it desirable to treat them at the same time. Perhaps *The Abel Family* is closest, among the published writings, to a traditional plot, but even this novel does not follow a straight line. It is the most traditional, too, in style and in narrative technique, if its two parts are considered individually, since each represents really only one time and a single narrative point of view. The first four chapters are of an introductory nature, narrated by an unidentified relative of the Abel family (who then disappears, for all practical purposes), while the second part constitutes the novel as such. The somewhat digressive first narrator presents the violent landscape, setting the scene with descriptions of the hostile surroundings of the village. George Wythe, in an article,[2] identifies the setting of *The Abel Family* as the "old Matute homestead," meaning the property of the novelist's maternal grandparents. There is in fact a high degree of coincidence in the description of the Ausejo home and that of the Abels, a "massive, square building," situated in "an isolated and gloomy spot, at the foot of the high mountains," with a deep *barranco* or break in the mountains behind it (the same *barranco* described in *The Dead Children, Celebration in the Northwest*, and some of the *Tales of Artámila*). And in both cases, there is the garden, the pasture or meadow, the orchard, and the grove of black poplars, with the whole enclosed by a dilapidated stone wall.

The narrator recalls the Abels when, as children together, he was fascinated and frightened by their strangeness. Years later, returning to the village, he rents their abandoned house and meets the village doctor, Eloy, who provides an outsider's view of the family, supplementing both the impressions of the narrator and the subjective and abruptly ended diary which constitutes the second part of the novel. Exploring the house, the narrator finds in a secret drawer the memoirs of Valba Abel, the elder daughter. This literary device whereby the author or one of his creations discovers the manuscript of a "true" story is familiar to all readers of *Don Quijote*. It was used in earlier times to give an air of increased credibility, but Matute has apparently employed it because it permits her to violate an essentially retrospective series of events via the present-tense perception of the narrator. In other words, it allows past to be experienced as present, increasing the interest and suspense. At the same time, the reader has the perspective of the present, in which the Abel family has disappeared, and this, reinforced by the frequent exclamations of horror and desperation with which Valba punctuates her memoirs, contributes to a mounting dread, in anticipation of an unhappy ending.

The memoirs begin at the moment when Valba, at fourteen, was recalled from boarding school because of her mother's death. The seven brothers and sisters are seen through her eyes and her descriptions, wherein tenderness and cruelty, hate and love are inextricably blended—just as in their relationships with each other. The four older brothers are quite sharply differentiated. Aldo, the eldest, brusque, ascetic, rigid, the hardworking and unpopular overseer of the family estate, conceals potential violence beneath his exterior hermetic insensibility. Gus, artistically inclined but weak and vacillating, lacks the perseverance to succeed either as violinist or painter (pursuits which had attracted Matute herself); he drinks too much and is unable to decide definitely on a career. Tito is charming, irresponsible, seemingly gay and full of life, but rather empty inside; egotistical, yet idealistic— Valba could never be sure whether he was the best or worst of her brothers. Juan, uninterested in either studying or the lands, indulges in fantastic, impossible projects; somewhat delicate and timid, he exasperates Aldo who abuses him and one day forces him to drink raw goat's milk from which he contracts a crippling fever. Embittered, he ultimately retreats from life to a monastery. Juan's sickness introduced the doctor, Eloy, who later falls in love with Valba. The two youngest children, not yet in school at the mother's death, are but little developed. Neglected and allowed to run wild, they are unenthusiastic students when finally sent to the city to school. Tavi, the youngest brother, scatter-brained, egotistical and conceited, eventually decides to enter the Naval Academy.

The younger sister, Octavia, thin, fragile, withdrawn, melancholy, a pathetic child robbed of childhood, serves to emphasize the irresponsibility of Valba and the older brothers, and to add to the number of links broken in the disintegration of the family. The father, Victor (soon removed), is ineffective, unable to control his strong-willed brood, and arouses more pity than respect. Each Abel (except Tavi, insufficiently developed for analysis) is, in his own way, radically alone, alienated from the rest of the family and the world at large, so that the group radiates solitude. Matute hereby achieves an overwhelming effect of estrangement, loneliness, and incommunication. This emotional atmosphere is reinforced by descriptions of the sullen, hostile village and unreceptive nature—violent storms, thirsty land, gigantic rocks, menacing sky, red mud, abrupt contrasts—the decaying, dark, ancient house, and the tone of bitter despair in which Valba writes. The peasants offer no relief to this, living at times almost like animals, more brutal than even their surroundings. So crushed by life that all they can do is manage the daily business of living, they seem unaware of or uninterested in any better existence.

The Abels, fairly prosperous provincial gentry, lived off the land, thanks to Aldo who administered their holdings and directed the workmen. As the principal, perhaps only landowners of the village, the family constituted a class apart, with the gulf between them and the peasants widened by the workmen's hatred for Aldo. The novel recounts the family's decadence and disintegration, the psychological development of Valba, and the constant conflicts between family members (the Cain and Abel theme). Given these characteristics, it may seem that *The Abel Family* represents a continuation of nineteenth-century Spanish regionalism, portraying life in rural Castile, or that it belongs in the category of the "novel of the soil" which appeared in Spain during the last century and has become still more prominent in the present one, with Andalusia the favorite setting. Then, too, during the sway of naturalism, the study of families was a popular choice, perhaps because it facilitated the presentation, simultaneously, of hereditary and environmental determinants. In this regard, there are moments when *The Abel Family* calls to mind an illustrious precedent from the close of the last century, Emilia Pardo Bazán's *Los pazos de Ulloa*, but this is only briefly.

The Abel Family has something of all these classifications, but its intent and emphasis are quite different. First, the novelist is concerned primarily not with local color, daily life in the region, or rural customs, but with human beings, personalities, and indirectly, the relation of these to historical events. She is interested in decadence not as proof of the effects of heredity and environment alone, but for its social implications, or in other words, also as a cause, as part of the total Spanish problem. Other themes, such as the radical solitude of the individual, the inability to communicate, alienation and despair, are frequent topics of existentialism and very much a phenomenon of the postwar period. A certain amount of caution is necessary, however, before calling any Spanish writer "existentialist," since the meaning in Spain is generally pejorative. The term has been abused, particularly by church-controlled critics and censors, until the present connotations are practically synonymous with "immoral," "sacrilegious," "atheistic," and the like. Suffice it to say, therefore, and with the object of avoiding this type of misunderstanding, that many themes of Matute are also constants of existentialism.

Dispersion of the Abel Family began when Tito became involved with liberals working in a nearby mine, and, implicated in a church burning (reflecting events just prior to the Civil War), had to leave town hurriedly. Gus went to the city, supposedly to paint, and lived a bohemian existence; he, too, was subsequently drawn into politics and jailed after causing a riot through his advocacy of socialistic land reform. Because of Tito's visits to the mine, the granddaughter of the mining engineer, Jacqueline, became Valba's friend, but returned to the city after falling in love with Tito. The Abels' father died, severing the last tenuous link which had held the family together. Valba took Octavia to a convent school in the city, and then decided not to return home. Without money, she went to stay with Jacqueline and her mother, Alicia, and so learned that Tito was having an affair with the latter, which drove the enamoured Jacqueline to return to the village and pursue Aldo, who was secretly in love with her. Valba, who had rejected Eloy's love because she was appalled by his dull, narrow existence, had an impulsive, somehow desperate affair with the much older Galo (Alicia's brother-in-law). Learning that he was leaving, she spent the night with him and begged him to take her along. Cast aside, humiliated and disillusioned, she returned to the village, and hysterically rejected Eloy's offer of marriage. Jacqueline spitefully married Aldo, forcing him to leave his beloved lands to live in the city, and Valba, left alone in the village, decided to sell the estate. She was prevented by the return of Tito, who stepped into Aldo's place as overseer.

Aldo appeared unexpectedly one night, having realized that Jacqueline still loved Tito, and the two brothers quarreled in a complex disagreement involving the girl, the land, and their mutual past; the dispute ended tragically when Aldo shot and killed Tito. Valba, at the narrative's end, wet her face with her brother's blood "as if it were a caress." This action seems slightly out of character, for Valba was not given to overt demonstrativeness or displays of emotion, which suggests a possible ritual or symbolic aspect. It enhances or heightens the sacrificial nature of the scene. The Aldo-Cain and Tito-Abel correspondence has been rather thoroughly prepared, with the sullen, withdrawn, hardworking but unloved personality of the one contrasting with the gay, carefree, favored indolence of the other. A well-known Spanish precedent comes to mind in this case also, and again it is in Miguel de Unamuno, with his treatment of the Cain and Abel theme in *Abel Sánchez,* a study of envy written some twenty years earlier. Unamuno's sympathies were definitely with Cain; Matute has retained a greater appearance of objectivity, but she has given him some very understandable motives.

The setting (the mountain village in Old Castile) is subsequently to become Matute's most frequent locale, and the descriptions, characteristic of her vision of this area, harmonize with those found in later works. Slightly stylized, with emphasis on the harshness of the landscape, the portrayal is nevertheless basically realistic—a realism verging on naturalism—in contrast to the idealized, indefinite, or imaginary locales of the juvenile works. It is true that occasional expressionistic elements intrude, as well, in the insistence upon the violent surroundings, and the primitivity of passions, but these are consistent with Matute's vision of Old Castile, conveying what she perceives to be the reality there. Perhaps oversimplifying, abstracting only land and sky, she uses in particular the colors of red and blue, with strongly contrasting light and shadow. In character description, there are noticeable several traits consistent with Matute's other writing. Valba, the most important personality, is typical of the novelist's female protagonists in that she is slightly stylized, but not at all idealized. She is no fictional beauty; quite the contrary, she is rather plain. In scattered references, the reader gleans that Valba is very dark, with intense eyes, but she is not attractive, and is small and childlike, with straight hair, and teeth like a young wolf's. This physical type—the girl with a boyish or childish body, straight hair, some other detail such as furnished in Valba's case by the teeth, and whose most important feature are her eyes—is the one preferentially employed by Matute. For the first time since some of the youthful stories in *Shybil's Review,*

Matute writes of a period which is recognizably the present, in-disputably anchored in concrete historical detail. *Little Theater*, while less specific, has sufficient ambientation to indicate the "modern" epoch, probably—but not necessarily—this century.

The concentration on the child and adolescent as the characters of prime importance, with ineffective or corrupt adults, as well as the numerous solitary and alienated personalities, are found in Matute's writing as a whole, both juvenilia and published works. And themes such as the tensions between landowners and peasants, the love for the land in some and in others the desperate desire to escape from the villages, the mixture of hate and love in family relationships, and the symbolic representation of the Civil War through the Cain and Abel image, will recur frequently in the novelist's future works. For the first time in her writings, there appear obvious vestiges of her childhood experiences in Mansilla, and, superimposed, events related to the Civil War, the apparent fruit of later investigations and discussions, since the sociological and other causative factors present in *The Abel Family* could not all be the result of early visits to rural Castile. While the social or concretely historical content of the novel may seem slender in comparison, for example, with a novel of Galdós, *The Abel Family* (in relation to her earlier works) is a decisive step in that direction. At the same time, it would seem to be Matute's first tentative exploration of causes underlying the Civil War, probed in greater depth in *The Fireflies, The Dead Children*, and her trilogy, *The Merchants*. Human variables predominate over the social, although it could be significant that all of the characters portrayed in any detail belong to the landowning class and have rather obvious faults. The economic factor has never been entirely absent from Matute's works, even the most fantastic, where money served as a concrete representation of materialism. In *The Abel Family* it has evolved to a closer association with social and historical factors and has acquired an increased capacity to influence human events, foreshadowing its future role in Matute's writing.

II   *The Next Few Years*

Until after the publication of her first book, Ana María Matute had met no professional writers. In her group of young intellectuals, all more or less of the same age, none could yet be considered a writer, and none carried sufficient weight to lead the others. Perhaps they all influenced each other through their discussions, their common interests and rebellion, their mutual stimulation. But outside their own circle, they were unknown, or they met with hostility, indifference, or silence:

Perhaps that group of adolescent writers who wrote in search of a road to truth in a vast sea of myths and shadows, of mirages and blindness—a road on which to shout their opposition, their hopes, and their still unanswered questions—should be called the group which hurled itself ("we splattered ourselves") against silence. A silence which clothed itself in indifference, a world which suffocated itself in cotton. A world which covered its ears and eyes, and which neither shouted nor whispered, but only repeated.

We searched. We went down to the docks, to the slums, to the shanty towns, to the taverns. We sought the pulse and heart of the people; we needed their words . . .
The silence increased, extended, and the youth, our friends, their backs turned to ideas, became excited only over football. The young people did not talk about literature or politics; they did not even know what it meant . . . . We did not exist. The few who read us either scolded us or treated us indulgently: we were the *enfants terribles* whom time would subdue. We would grow and turn to "normal" literature and "normal" ways.[3]

It was truly a time which required unswerving vocation and dedication of a writer, for in Spain this occupation could offer neither artistic nor economic satisfactions: the censor's restrictions and mutilations excluded beforehand any sense of artistic achievement, and the near-total lack of reading public offered little possibility of financial reward. The situation has been a long while in improving, and the censorship, although somewhat relaxed in recent years, continues very much in existence, and the market for fiction in Spain is still extremely small. Many contemporary Spanish writers are much better known outside the country than within. Ana María Matute and those of her generation who continued to write in the face of these obstacles did so because their need to speak out was independent of both the dangers and the rewards.

During the course of 1951, the novelist began work on *The Dead Children*, a massive novel of over five hundred pages and the longest of her works to date, the completion of which was to require seven years. Her work was often interrupted by events in her personal life and by economic pressures which forced her to complete and publish other, shorter works to supplement her income. Also in 1951, *The Abel Family* was translated to Italian, and Ana María received her first literary prize—by no means a major one—for a short story, "No hacer nada" ("Doing Nothing").[4] Consisting of fifteen pesetas (less than twenty-five cents at the present exchange, although then it was somewhat more), the prize was awarded by the "Tertulia Café del Turia." A *tertulia* is a peculiarly Spanish institution, an informal gathering of people with some common interest (which may be art or football, literature or bullfights), meeting at regular intervals and in the same place. This was a literary *tertulia* which met in the Café del Turia in Barcelona. The following year, the novelist received a similar but more prestigious award, the "Premio Café Gijón." The Café Gijón in Madrid has for several years been the meeting place of some of Spain's most important artistic and literary figures, and considerable intellectual respectability is attached to their yearly selection of the novelette to be recognized by the Café Gijón Prize. *Celebration in the Northwest*, most artistically perfect of Matute's early works, received this distinction in 1952.

The novelist has said that she never intended to marry, that she was not born for marriage, and could not visualize herself married; but nevertheless, in November, 1952, she married Ramón Eugenio de Goicoechea,[5] another writer, and almost immediately, "life became complicated and strange." E. García Luengo, a contemporary Spanish novelist and journalist who knew the couple, and who was a member of the jury which awarded the "Premio Café Gijón" to *Celebration in the Northwest*, has described Matute's husband in these words: "I met Ramón Eugenio de Goicoechea as a bachelor, about the year 1948 or 1949, when the ingenuous desire of attracting attention forced him to certain extravagant activities. In another, I would qualify this pretension as roguish or twisted . . . [but] Goicoechea had something helpless, a sort of vital awkwardness and trembling affectiveness that made him suffer. . . . Within his picturesqueness, I thought I could perceive a man burned and destroyed by his own farce, for which reason it was no longer a farce."[6] Elsewhere in the same article, mention is made of Goicoechea's "slightly innocent and overly serious effrontery and sarcasm" and his "abstract, juvenile pessimism." It should be emphasized that the general tone of the article was cordial, sympathetic, even friendly, and that the references elsewhere to Goicoechea, both oral and printed, have been considerably less kind. In García Luengo's summary, it was his estimation that Goicoechea had "enormous literary gifts," but was overly impressionistic and tended too much to the picturesque and the dramatic.

Various literary acquaintances of the couple have referred to occasions when journalists or scholars interviewing Ana María Matute were interrupted by her husband who took over the conversation to talk of his own works. It seems that his personality was not one to adapt easily to her greater fame. García Luengo likewise indicates that this may have been a problem: "On another occasion, Goicoechea read us a chapter of his unfinished novel. . . . Afterward, I commented that the general tone of the narration, what you might call the style, reminded me of his wife's. It seems that Ramón Eugenio did not care for my opinion."[7] It should be emphasized that this article predates considerably the breakup of the marriage, and therefore constitutes not speculation as to causes for the separation, but simply the observations of an informed outsider.

Matute has avoided all mention of her marriage or of her life during these years, and has maintained almost complete silence regarding her husband, but the relationship seems to have been unhappy from a very early date. The personality problems, obvious apparently even to the casual observer, were complicated by the literary rivalry and the fact that in Spain it is more difficult perhaps than in many other places for a man to accept being overshadowed by his wife. The "emancipation" of women is recent in Spain (and by no means complete), and there is great psychological resistance to a woman's being anything but a housewife and mother. Women are resented as competitors, and more so if successful. Another cause of difficulty seems to have been that Goicoechea was either incompetent or irresponsible financially. He handled his wife's business matters, but left bills unpaid so long that her author's rights and royalties were on the point of being embargoed and even personal property seized. She was forced to assume personal responsibility for enormous debts he had contracted in her name—in a country where a woman cannot even have a bank account without her husband's authorization.

Shortly after their marriage, the couple moved to Madrid. Matute found herself obliged to attend many literary *tertulias* with her husband, but these, in contrast to the discussions with her group in Barcelona, bored her terribly. The one positive result was that during these years she became acquainted with nearly all the Spanish writers of the day, and began to gain in familiarity with the literary scene beyond the national borders, first through conversations, and then expanded readings once translations began to enter Spain. The intuitive and purely personal writer matured and evolved rapidly as a reaction to this exposure.

CHAPTER 4

Pequeño Teatro *and Juan Pablo*

NOT LONG after moving to Madrid, the novelist decided to make another effort to publish the half-forgotten manuscript of *Pequeño teatro (Little Theater)*. She reworked it without altering the plot or other essentials: "Chapter for chapter, it is the same, exactly the same. I only polished the style, perfecting it grammatically, or what I supposed was perfecting it."[1] The revised manuscript was entered in the contest for the "Premio Planeta" (now Spain's most heavily endowed literary award) and won the prize, which included publication. Thus *Little Theater* appeared in print in 1954, eleven years after it was written. Despite its prize-winning debut, however, the novel never found favor with Spanish critics or readers.

Ana María Matute's only child, Juan Pablo, was born in that same year, 1954. Her son would henceforth be an increasingly important element in her life, and a compensation for numerous matrimonial trials. "I made a mistake," she observed. "but with him, because of him—it isn't a mistake, either,"[2] As the boy grew, she spent hours playing with him, entering into his games, and joining in his fantasies. Soon she began inventing stories for him. Combined with her own youthful interest in children's fiction and her unpleasant memories of the dull, "instructive" exempla served to juvenile readers in Spain, what had begun as entertainment for her son subsequently carried Matute into new literary ventures, writing for children. A reform or renewal of juvenile fiction in Spain during the past decade is attributable in considerable measure to the interest taken by major writers in younger readers, and Matute has been a pioneer in the effort to produce works truly attuned to children's tastes. She has written for several different juvenile age levels, advancing roughly in the same measure as her son has grown.

I Little Theater

The first of Matute's published novels in chronological order of composition, *Little Theater* has a setting unique among her works, a Basque fishing village and summer resort on Spain's northern Atlantic (or Cantabrian) coast. While she was less familiar with this area than with Madrid, Barcelona, or Mansilla, the novelist had some acquaintance with the region and environment portrayed. *Little Theater* was written shortly after she spent some time in a similar village, vacationing with her family a few years after the end of the war. The name "Oiquixa" is fictitious and the area not specifically identified, but the Basque names and occasional dialectical words are sufficient indication. One recent article identifies the setting of *Little Theater* as corresponding "to the fishing village of Zumaya—with its steep streets rising from the wharves, an old lighthouse dominating a bluff, and the heavy waves of the Bay of Biscay plunging like racing horses against the rocks." [3] The same source notes that Matute visited this coast on several occasions as a girl in the company of her mother's old Basque servant-companion. The novelist thus would have had more than a superficial acquaintance with the locale. Insofar as setting is concerned, then, *Little Theater* represents a transitional stage between the exotic or fantastic backgrounds chosen for her juvenilia, and the areas best known to Matute in which her mature novels are set.

As in the works written earlier, no exact time is specified; likewise, there is a lack of identifiable historical events or correlatives. However, such details as the mention of the King's visit and the length of dresses worn suggest the first or second decade of this century. A vague air of modernity is conveyed by the attitudes and themes, although not reinforced by concrete detail. In this respect, too, *Little Theater* must be considered transitional. It is not timeless, as is a large part of her juvenile production, but neither is it set in the historical present, the period of the novelist's own lifetime. While specific dates were lacking in *The Abel Family* also (and such will be the case with some of her later writing), no doubt as to its precise historical context is possible.

Not only are the physical and temporal settings transitional; *Little Theater* also marks the change between the fantastic characters and events of much of Matute's earlier works and the pronounced realistic nature of what is written thereafter. *Little Theater* contains a combination of the realistic and the fantastic, noted by various critics. Presumably lacking knowledge of her juvenilia, however, they failed to perceive the transition, a task further complicated by the non-chronological appearance of the novel. Eugenio de Nora [4] describes *Little Theater* as "Not entirely fantastic but lacking verisimilitude, confusing and with vague outlines, vitalized almost exclusively by what it contains of anguished erotic elegy of adolescence." He considers the characters and situations "rather the figures of hallucination than a possible real world." Alborg [5] assumes with little support that Matute was attempting in this novel to combine her peculiar, lyrical style with the techniques of *objetivismo* (Objectivism), in fashion when the critic wrote, but not when *Little Theater* was drafted some fifteen years previously. When the novel is viewed in the context of Matute's total work, earlier and later, the process of transition stands out clearly.

"Oiquixa" is an archetypal small provincial town, where almost nothing ever happens, so that any break in the monotony is eagerly welcomed; it is one of those towns where almost everyone knows everyone else, and gossip, malice, and hypocrisy are major occupations. Its morality is narrow and traditional, its politics reactionary, its entertainments all but nonexistent. Mass, "charity," and talking constitute the only distractions approved for women of the "better" families. The town is in large part the property of one man, a self-made millionaire, Kepa Devar, proprietor of stores, canneries, the cement factory, and the coal business, and builder of the orphanage, the hospital, and the Hotel Devar. This hotel, unnecessarily large, ostentatious, and usually empty, satisfied Kepa as a symbol, as well as because the King once stayed there. However, as is the case with most adults (and particularly the wealthy ones) in Matute's work, Kepa is not happy, despite his financial success. His life is empty of personal and subjective values; ethically he is not too admirable, despite his philanthropy; and while many envy and flatter him, no one really likes him. Kepa is almost totally alone, frustrated even in his triumphs, lonely, unappreciated, and unshared. Like many a Matute character, he often drank too much. His wife (who never loved him) died shortly after the birth of their daughter, Zazu. Communication and expressions of affection between Kepa and his daughter are most infrequent; both are solitary, isolated, alienated.

Zazu represents a revolt against the proper, traditional, conventional behavior expected of the provincial young lady. Refusing to conform in appearance and to join in the activities of other girls of her class, she frequently escapes to the lower-class harbor quarter, there apparently running wild. Her affairs with sailors and fishermen, in which nymphomania is insinuated, were the scandal of Oiquixa, whose women treated her with hypocritical flattery but talked viciously of her in private. Zazu, having found neither love nor satisfaction in her desperate search, is prematurely embittered. Her maiden aunts Eskarne and Mirentxu (extremes in hypocrisy and conformity) have betrothed her to a much older sea captain whom Zazu has never met. To her approaching matrimony, as to most other things, Zazu is apparently indifferent.

The novel is related from a variety of perspectives, minimizing use of the objective narrator, recounting events from within the subjectivity of various characters (a sort of interior monologue which frequently contrasts with external words or actions), and containing occasional comment by various other characters as to what has actually happened. This is the first of Matute's works which can be considered, in a meaningful sense, an experiment in narrative technique or point of view. While perhaps not entirely successful, inasmuch as at moments events are obscure, ambivalent, or confusing, nevertheless it is a most important stage in her artistic maturation. It should be noted that that very obscurity constitutes, for some readers, one of the novel's principal charms, adding an air of mystery and magic quite in keeping with the atmosphere of the puppet show which serves as central symbol.

Little Theater is a novel in which there are frequently two or more possible interpretations of events, although the author supplies some evidence or clues which help the reader to reach a specific conclusion. Her refusal to impose her own particular interpretation, or to evaluate, comment, and moralize anticipates tenets of the Objectivist movement, imported to Spain from France at approximately the time of the novel's appearance in print. The coincidence is interesting, but the general atmosphere and symbolic nature of the work are very different from that of the typical Objectivist fiction.

One of the novel's "perspectives" and major characters is Ilé Eroriak, an orphaned adolescent. This strange, often fantastic personality lives on scraps, and sleeps by turns on the beach and on a shelf with the worn-out marionettes of the old hunchback puppeteer, Anderea—the only person to treat Ilé with true kindness. Ilé drinks too much whenever he earns a few coins unloading boats. He is considered crazy and often made a laughingstock. Events told as he perceived them are at times deformed by a mixture of imagination and incomprehension; nevertheless, Ilé and old Anderea have sensitivity and insights which the more normal villagers have not.

In addition to Ilé, there is at least one other principal narrator, an anonymous, objective voice outside the boy's consciousness and not identified with any of the other characters. For lesser periods of time, the narration is done from within the consciousness of Zazu, Kepa and that of the adventurer, Marco; and there are momentary glimpses of the interior of some minor characters. This shifting point of view recalls briefly the technique of multiple perspectives used by another important Spanish writer in this century, Pérez de Ayala. The difference is that Matute does not present varying complementary versions of her narrative, but instead uses the differing perspectives in more fragmentary fashion. In other words, while Pérez de Ayala employs multiple perspectives to show varying views of one and the same thing or event, Matute uses these perspectives in succession, projecting from varying points of view different but related things or events. Occasionally two views of the same event are found in *Little Theater* and these constitute the clues with which the reader must construct a unitary whole from the various fragmentary perspectives.

The action of the novel concerns one break in the routine monotony of Oiquixa, beginning with the arrival of an exotic and mysterious stranger, Marco, and ending with his departure. It slowly becomes apparent that Marco is a former convict, a small-scale adventurer and swindler, apparently a pathological liar who believes his own inventions: he tells dozens of contradictory stories about his birth and youth, and most of them move him to tears. Marco also seems to be a manic depressive, going frequently from extreme exaltation to the depths of despair, and alternating between considering himself superhuman and godlike, or abjectly inferior. Despite all this, his picturesque eccentricity and verbal magic, cleverly planted rumors and aura of greatness, eventually fool everyone but Zazu. She sees him for what he is and hates him, yet simultaneously feels a fatal attraction for him. Rejecting and humiliating him, she is nevertheless unable to resist following him and repeatedly resuming their relationship. Marco, knowing that she has never loved, determines to capture her heart in vengeance for her rejection and then abandon her.

Marco befriended Ilé and spent much of his time with him, even leaving the comfort of the Hotel Devar to sleep with him on the steps of the church. This strange conduct caused only admiration among the townspeople, who believed Marco to be enormously wealthy and powerful but bored with his worldly existence. Convincing Oiquixa society that Ilé was a latent genius, Marco appealed to the provincial desire for local glory and suggested a great collection to finance Ilé's education, whereby all might share in the honor of having discovered the future marvel. In the sudden competition over the formerly abused and neglected Ilé, Matute satirizes that false charity given either for the sake of appearance or because it promises some benefit for the giver. Marco's plan was to escape with the funds the day after the collection, taking Ilé with him. Expecting Zazu to follow him, he sent Ilé to inform her of his departure. Zazu realized that she could no longer escape Marco; she was in love for the first time, and he had become somehow part of her. She knew also that Marco would humiliate and destroy her, and this her pride would not allow. Unable to remain at home, struggling against conflicting emotions as she apparently set out to join Marco, Zazu (by accident or design) walked off the end of the breakwater and drowned herself. Marco's hysterical, cowardly reaction disillusioned Ilé, who previously idolized him, and he denounced Marco to the police.

The "little theater" of the title may be either the puppet theater of old Anderea, or Oiquixa itself, wherein the inhabitants are like marionettes, impelled by forces and emotions over which they have no control.[6] In a larger sense, the title could apply to all of Spain, for the hypocrisy and narrow conformity portrayed are characteristic of provincial society as a whole. Applying the symbol most broadly, the "little theater" could be the world ("All the world's a stage"), with mankind seen as a group of actors or puppets. In this same vein, the scenery is often compared to theatrical backdrops or to painted paper, and the characters referred to (by other characters, the narrator, and themselves) as puppets, wooden figures, dolls, and the like. Zazu, Marco, Ilé, and Anderea, in particular, frequently describe themselves or others as marionettes. There is likewise an insistent accumulation of comparisons of characters and events to fantasies and dreams.

Still further blurring the exact line of demarcation between illusion and reality, some of the conversations between Marco and Anderea, and later Anderea and Ilé, suggest that none of the book is happening, or that nothing has happened in reality, that everything is a fabrication in the mind of the old puppeteer. Matute thereby achieves an atmosphere of farce and artificiality which serves her admirably in exposing the conventionality and hypocrisy of the archetypal small town which caused her to write *Little Theater*. The extent to which this device succeeded is evinced by the fact that Spanish critics have without exception failed to see the significance of the work, or to perceive its satiric social criticism.

The use of the little theater motif is frequent in Matute's work, recurring in several short stories; in the collections of memoirs and autobiographical essays, *The River*, and *Halfway Down the Road*, and in novels such as *Celebration in the Northwest* and *First Memoirs*. More than just an insistent literary device, this reflects one of the novelist's lifelong interests. From the days when as a child she operated her own puppet theater, and feverishly attended the performances of similar theaters in the parks of Madrid and Barcelona, or watched, spellbound, the enactments by strolling players in the village square of Mansilla, Matute has felt the fascination of these survivals of the *commedia dell' arte,* the marionettes, and the improvised performances.

Little Theater offers a particularly fruitful area for a study of Matute's style, much more than is the case with *The Abel Family* (possibly because the latter book is limited by the use of the diary, presumably written without literary pretensions, or because it appeared at a stage in the novelist's career when she was particularly subject to external influences which were at variance with her own personal style). While nearly everything Matute has written has an almost unmistakable ring, her style appears much more uninhibitedly lyric in some works than others, where the nature of the subject matter itself may restrain or restrict the expression.

Characteristic of the novelist is an emphasis on the eyes and hair of her juvenile protagonists, and a predilection for rather boyish, childlike, and not too attractive girls. The description of Zazu typifies these traits, and illustrates a number of other Matute stylistic devices:

In Zazu's eyes there was some incomprehensible excessiveness. In Zazu's eyes there was too much childhood and too much boredom. Zazu's pupils were a diaphanous crystal, a bottomless, infinite crystal. Zazu was preoccupied by her eyes. She was preoccupied by her face. She was always looking at herself in the mirror. Zazu's life was filled with long periods of nothing to do, and in the house on that sad and inhospitable Nagusia Street, in the town suffocated beneath murmurings and suspicions, beneath that heavy, densely gray sky with its particles of soot, fog and malicious conversations, Zazu closed herself in with her mirror. She looked at her face with its tanned skin and wide-open eyes, where the round centers of the pupils, black and shining like pinheads, fixed themselves painfully on her gaze. Then Zazu know that everything in her might have been perfect and that nothing was.[7]

The parallel construction of the first two sentences, and of the fourth and fifth, as well as the repetition of words and phrases, typify many Matute descriptions. Similarly, within sentences, parallel or bipartite constructions are frequent. The novelist also has a special predilection for tripartite constructions within sentences, or a series of three adjectives or other descriptive elements, and both can be found in the long seventh sentence, beginning with "in the house." Metaphorical descriptions of physical or tangible objects in terms of qualitative, intangible elements (possibly adapted from Lorca) also abound in Matute, as seen in the "densely gray sky with its particles of soot, fog and malicious conversations." The novelist's fondness for contrast and antithesis is suggested by the last sentence and clearly shown in a passage a few pages later which mentions the other girls of Zazu's age and class, their words "overflowing with malign innocence." [8] Another favorite Matute device is synesthesia, repeatedly used in the same paragraph to describe the girls' dresses "of bright colors . . . like violent shrieks, yellow, red, green, in the dense, morning stroll . . . like sad, languid, useless cries, blue rose, mauve in the evening stroll. . . " The effect of muted, smothered protest which is conveyed in addition to the actual description is admirably suited to expression of the conventional, hypocritical atmosphere in which Zazu lives. Matute has stated that her procedure is instinctive or intuitive rather than deliberate, that she does consciously set out to achieve certain predetermined effects by stylistic means. If the often admirable integration of form and content is not the result of design, it must be explained by an unusual degree of artistic sensitivity.

CHAPTER 5

Las luciérnagas *and* En esta tierra

SHORTLY AFTER the birth of her son, the novelist's severe financial straits made urgent the need to publish something immediately. While already deeply involved in her work on *Los hijos muertos (The Dead Children)*, this novel was far from completion, and at the moment she had only the manuscript of the previously censored *Las luciérnagas (The Fireflies)*. Fighting her disgust at what she considered a sacrifice of principle, she decided to compromise and rewrite the novel. The new version included extensive revisions, and an entirely different ending, with sweeping changes made in the crucial third and final part. In its rewritten form, entitled *En esta tierra (In This Land)*, the novel was licensed by the censors and appeared in print in 1955. Its success has been limited, and Matute has always considered it inferior to the original version. Eugenio de Nora *(La novela española contemporánea*, II, ii, 295) mentions that the novel in its earlier form was a semifinalist for the 1949 Premio Nadal, which would place its composition prior to that of *Celebration in the Northwest*. The failure in this competition and the subsequent difficulties of the original manuscript with the censorship thus fall in the same period when the novelist was beginning work on *The Dead Children* and may well be directly related to similarities with the later novel. Partly because of her low opinion of the altered narrative, and partly because of her emotional reaction to the censoring, she has never had the least fondness for *In This Land*. "I don't like that novel at all; I hate it," she stated in a 1965 interview; "I am in no way satisfied with it." The unfortunate novel seems also to have become associated in her mind with a long chain of unhappy events of a personal nature which began at about the same period and would eventually culminate in her divorce.

I   *The Novels*

Since the two titles, despite extensive changes, represent essentially one creative effort or inspiration, they may be treated as a unit. *In This Land* is the published and more accessible version, so preference must be given to it. This is the first of Matute's novels to use Barcelona as a setting, and to be specifically situated in a definite period of time, the Spanish Civil War. It is relatively more objective than earlier works, with the narrative presented more directly. The perspective is broadened to include not merely a village, but a far broader range of characters, groups, and socio-economic phenomena. When compared with the earlier novels, individual personalities and psychologies seem to have become less important, with many personages now notable more for what they represent (as members of the bourgeoisie, of the Socialist Party, of the proletariat, etc.). It may be for this reason that many of them are rather vague and nebulous, their sentiments ill-defined (as is the case with Cristian), or that they tend to be stereotyped (Cloti, Soledad's mother, the elder Barral).

While not one of Matute's better works, *In This Land* is by no means the worst. It is among the most political of her writings, and definitely the most audacious up until the time of its publication. *In This Land* has been relatively neglected by the critics, perhaps because the subject treated was still extremely touchy when the novel appeared, or perhaps (since the Spanish literary world is fairly small) it was rather widely known that the published work was very much a compromise and it was not considered entirely fair to base a judgment on it. The few critical mentions it did receive have shown a certain ambivalence. Eugenio de Nora *(loc. cit.)* considers the characters "when not strange, eccentric or mysterious, or subject to a stereotyped pattern; in any case, much less representative and alive than they should have been." Nevertheless, he does not deny the novel a certain "testimonial and artistic force." He concludes however that the reader's "dominant impression is an overwhelming, perplexed uncertainty as to the meaning" of events. The kindest opinion of *In This Land* is that of J. L. Alborg *(Hora actual de la novela española,* Madrid, 1958), who attributes to it "indisputable human interest and intensity [and] great descriptive force and plasticity." Writing shortly before the appearance of *The Dead Children*, he considered *In This Land* Matute's "most complete success" to date, despite his opinion that it contained obvious defects of style such as overloading and overemphasis, a loss of tone and shadings in favor of painting in more violent colors (pp. 184–187).

For the scholar, this novel is interesting in its anticipation of many of the social and political themes of *The Dead Children*, the necessary link between her earlier works and that major novel. Without the intermediate stage constituted by *The Fireflies* and *In This Land*, there would be a tremendous gulf between *The Dead Children* and the writings published previously. Here for the first time in Matute's work there appears a passionate defense of the humble and dispossessed, a cry for understanding the causes underlying the revolt of the lower classes, the implicit but fervent sympathy with the losers in the Civil War (a category which also embraces a large share of the "winners").

The social panorama includes the protagonist's typical bourgeois family; the modest family of refugees, with their Socialist daughter; the intellectual accused of treason and eliminated by his political comrades; the gang of delinquents; an anarchist political commissar and former village schoolteacher; the hostile, aggressive, semi-anonymous proletariat, and many more. From the perspective of social comprehensiveness, this is Matute's most ambitious undertaking up to the date of its publication, and second only to *The Dead Children* in scope.

It might be argued that there are autobiographical elements here, since the protagonist shares with the novelist a similar age (although she is a few years older at the time of the outbreak of the Civil War in 1936), similar family background, upbringing, and social status. The apparently average daughter of a bourgeois family, Soledad senses that she is different; she feels estranged, in rebellion against the things expected of her in the *colegio* and at home. Her father (like Matute's) is a Barcelona industrialist; however, the fictional father is murdered—executed for class reasons—and the family forced to live under difficult conditions, with insufficient food and with part of their house requisitioned by the working-class parties as quarters for a lower-class refugee family from Madrid. Their daughter, Cloti, Soledad's age but in many ways her opposite, seems to belong largely to the naturalistic tradition and is probably intended to appear as a victim of the environment and circumstances in which she has lived, exposed to hunger and vice from an early age. Cloti is not a sympathetic creation: she is coarse, uneducated, uncouth, and prematurely debauched.

Soledad's brother, a cold, solitary egotist, had spent most of his time before the war engaged in sports, or in bed, reading. During the war, he turned to looting in the streets after bombing raids, and so became involved with a gang led by Daniel Barral, a boy of his own age, mortally ill with tuberculosis. With Eduardo's absence, and because of the family's difficult situation, Soledad took a teaching job arranged by her former tutor, Ramón Boloix, who had become politically influential. She later abandoned the job profoundly revulsed after he attempted to make love to her. One night, knowing that Daniel was dying, and terrified by the thought of death, Eduardo convinced Soledad to accompany him to the Barral home, where she met Daniel's older brother, Cristián. In this night while Daniel died, a bombing raid destroyed the building, killing the father and Pablo, eldest of the three Barral boys. Eduardo disappeared and Soledad was left along with Cristián in the burning city.

Superimposed on the primary narrative is another, told in flash-backs. Pablo, trapped and dying in the wreckage of the building, recalls his life, beginning with the time when the three Barral boys were abandoned by their mother who ran away with a traveling perfume salesman—a blow from which their father, a quiet, unworldly scholar and dreamer, never recovered. The father's teaching salary was meagre, and Pablo was forced to work in a slaughterhouse while he continued his studies, finally succeeding after long struggle in becoming a teacher. Embittered and brutalized by his first assignment to a forgotten village in Extremadura, he obtained transfer to a factory town, where he became involved in the early stages of revolution, leading a local manifestation. His concern for social justice was clearly an effort to avenge injustices in his own life, and Pablo's rise in the leftist hierarchy left him restless and dissatisfied. He became fairly powerful in his party and lived well, but was disillusioned and discontented. Pablo realizes as he is dying that he will never enter the "promised land."

Leaving the scene of the bombing and deaths of the rest of the Barral family, Cristián and Soledad went to a large house in the suburbs of Barcelona where Pablo had been living, remaining there for an indefinite length of time and becoming lovers. They continued living in the house until arrested and separated. When released, after some time in jail, Soledad realized she was pregnant. She finally located Cristián and convinced him to come home with her, but as they turned toward what might have been a new life, Franco's army entered Barcelona. Cristián ran toward them, unarmed and shouting, and was shot. In this version of the novel Cristián's ideas and ideals are never too clear. Apparently he was a draft dodger, and had subsequently deserted when forced to defend the Republic, but he seems to have been indifferent to the insurgents as well. Critics have protested that the end of the novel leaves the reader in doubt as to whether his final shout was one of joy or despair at the arrival of the Nationalists, but this ambiguity is undoubtedly due largely to the censorship.

The typescript of *The Fireflies* shows only minor differences with relation to the published counterpart during the early stages. An occasional paragraph has been cut, sentences or words are missing, but the essentials of the two versions coincide substantially up to the point that Soledad and Cristián meet. Certain nonessentials differ: for example, Cloti is called Celia in the earlier version, and the family of the three brothers is named not Barral, but Soto. Cristián has very explicit prior prison experience and tends to be more philosophical. He speaks in almost existential terms of human limits, the desire to go beyond them, and asserts that prison is in the most meaningful sense internal, inescapable: "I am the prison." He questions the value of struggling, of life itself, having lost his beliefs, but emphatically does not want to die. The suffering of individuals in war, the tremendous intellectual and emotional as well as physical tolls, emerge perhaps still more clearly than in *In This Land*, but there is nothing which can be called partisanship. Those who suffer most, on both sides, are those who suffer always, the weak, the old, the poor, the very young. Cristián clearly expresses the novelist's own view when he affirms: "War is a macabre farce which achieves nothing, betters nothing."[1]

The deterministic influence of the poverty-stricken early years of Pablo[2] is more extensively and explicitly presented in *The Fireflies*, as is the genesis of his confused rebellion. More clearly than in *In This Land*, a parallel emerges between Pablo and Cristián, one an activist, the other evasive, but both victims of the impossible gulf between their ideals and the reality in which they live. In the published version, much of a social nature has been edited out of the life story of Pablo, both his reflections and actual experiences. Notable by its absence is a section containing Pablo's memories of the isolated village where he was destined as a rural schoolmaster, passages reminiscent of Baroja,[3] emphasizing the primitive morality or almost bestial sexuality of the inhabitants, the suppressed passions and suffocating atmosphere of religious repression and superstition, the physical and spiritual backwardness, the substandard health and education, and the frequent incidence of mental retardation. The brutalizing effect of life in the villages upon the rural schoolteachers is a frequent theme with Matute, but perhaps nowhere so forcefully presented as in this censored narrative. Pablo, involved in an elemental love affair repugnant to his own sensibility, turns to drinking incessantly, eating like an animal, attempting to annihilate feeling and time.

Also largely censored is the next episode of his life in a provincial town where Pablo experiences the existence of the working class, acquires a social conscience, and encounters a cause: Humanity. In the lower-class bar he frequents, he comes in contact with anarchists and socialists, begins to read Kropotkin, and to visit the homes of the proletariat, who are helpless against the established order. Somewhat unexpectedly, he finds himself a social and political activist, participating in the move to liberate by force certain workers imprisoned for the execution of a hated manager. This rather long section, and that dealing with the popular revolution which follows, quite explicit in descriptions of physical violence, gory vengeance, and elemental passion, are, not surprisingly, omitted in the published version. While some parts may have been found morally objectionable by the Spanish censor, it is obvious that what has been most consistently eliminated deals with the frustrations, inequities, and grievances motivating the violence by the lower-class parties in the Civil War. The exact manner of Pablo's death, by his own hand, is also somewhat masked in the published version. Trapped in the rubble of the bombed building, mortally injured, and in great pain but presumably hours from death, he shoots himself in *The Fireflies*. Suicide is considered unacceptable morally and religiously by the official Catholic censors, and would perhaps be even more so in this case because Pablo is consistently presented as tired of life and searching for peace, so that death attracts him as a sort of promised land.

While the changes and deletions in the story of Pablo are considerable, the greatest difference between the two novels comes later, after Cristián and Soledad have been released from prison, and have subsequently located each other; this was after his forcible mobilization and escape from the army defending Barcelona. In the published version, the story ends almost immediately with his death; in *The Fireflies* the two marry after the end of the war and struggle interminably against the hopeless postwar economic and political situation until at last Cristián is driven by the need to provide medicine for a sick baby to attempt robbery and murder, for which he is condemned to prison and subsequently sent to a work camp. The events leading up to his desperate outburst of violence, as well as the life led by himself, Soledad, and their son in the years of his imprisonment emphasize two things: the near-impossibility of the survival of ideals and idealists in the postwar jungle, and the everwidening gap between generations.

Both Pablo and Cristián are idealists, however different their ideals and modes of expression, and they coincide in the inability to accept or adapt to the circumstances in which they live. Both meet disillusionment, and their fates symbolize the death of ideals, in the one case with the physical death of Pablo, in the other with the near-disintegration of Cristián and the obvious lack of suitability and viability of ideals for the situations and problems he must meet. Without any sacrifice of verisimilitude, Matute's painting of life in the immediate postwar years suggests repeatedly that those idealists who died were the lucky ones. The others live to see the slow crumbling of the things in which they have believed (and fought for in many cases), for which the entire country struggled and suffered, and for which untold thousands died.

The ideals of Pablo were largely collective, those of Cristián, individual and personal. The former may symbolize collective or social aspirations destroyed or dispersed in the war and the fall of the Republic; the latter those individual shreds of hope or idealism remaining after the end of the conflict. Cristián's ideals are comparatively modest: he wants only to live honestly, in peace and decency, independently, to work without favors or favoritism, but with hope of progress. Significantly, both he and Soledad have remained essentially uncommitted during the war, despite their own (opposing) class origins and the involvements of members of their families in partisan sentiment or activity. They welcome the end of the war as the end to an intolerable situation, a chance to begin anew, accepting the long hard task of building a life for themselves in a country in ruins. Almost totally apolitical, their attitude toward the victors seems to have two principal components: gratitude for the end of hostilities, and a guarded optimism. Young, moderately ambitious, willing to work, they ask nothing of the new regime but a chance to live by their own honest and unaided efforts. It is precisely this, however, which proves to be impossible in postwar Spain.

Inflation, black-market chicanery, favoritism, the buying and selling of recommendations, scarcities, general and widespread corruption are such that almost daily evidence accumulates indicating that honesty and scruples are an insurmountable handicap. Six years pass in which Soledad and Cristián work ever harder, living ever more modestly, but find themselves progressively more deeply in debt and with fewer job opportunities available. Cristián's years of study to become a doctor are but a useless sacrifice, as at the end he cannot pay the cost of receiving his degree, and even less establish a practice. They are surrounded by the success of others, often uneducated, unscrupulous; debts, humiliations, and problems accumulate that cannot be fought with pride, hope, and idealism. Threatened with eviction, unable to buy food and medicine for his son, Cristián stabs a moneylender.

The prison camp to which he is sent is one in which the convicts may shorten their sentences by working. Like similar camps which appear in *The Dead Children*, Matute's memoirs, and several short stories, it has as its model the prison work camp constructed near the novelist's grandmother's house in Mansilla de la Sierra, where she spent her summers as a child. Matute has often mentioned the impression caused her by the women, wives of the prisoners for the most part, who came with their children to live nearby, often in improvised shacks or hovels, where they might catch sight of their men and speak to them an hour on Sundays. Soledad appears in this role in the closing pages of *The Fireflies*, leading her six-year-old-son. The child's question, asking a definition of fireflies, reveals indirectly the meaning of the title: "They are poor things, half worm, half butterfly, always falling, with their heads alight."[4] Soledad seems to be unaware of the symbolic plane on which this description fits her and Cristián, but it is clear that the novelist intends it to apply not only to them, but to the idealist in general. The last lines refer to a falling star, recalling an earlier scene of hope and optimism shortly after Soledad and Cristián are reunited, in which the sky is also filled with stars. The contrast is heightened by the intervening six years of slowly destroyed illusions, with the symbolic denunciation underscored by Matute's use of the falling star motif (death) from the early juvenilia on. No direct reference to the national political and economic situation is needed: it is present in innumerable factors which weigh on the protagonists. A frequent truism is that you can kill the thinker but not the idea; *The Fireflies* demonstrates that there are things more fatal for ideals than death. This would also seem to be supported by a comparison with the "milder" published version, *In This Land*. Apparently the novelist found no other way to make a comparably powerful presentation of the extent of the disappointment of Cristián in the new regime than to have the first encounter result directly in his death.

Stylistically, there are many similarities to *Little Theater*, although the tone is much less lyric and the air of fantasy and unreality has been almost totally suppressed, except for isolated moments when the novelist wishes to convey that occasionally hallucinatory air that real events may assume in moments of crisis or stress. The same techniques may be employed—repetition, parallel construction, the series of three adjectives or descriptive elements—but the effect achieved is different: "A world that was viscous and ugly surrounded her. A world where reality was fear, failure, clumsiness. A world of larvas and worms, fighting desperately for a beautiful, impossible, distant form. A world where there was no place for her."[5] The novelist has begun to employ more frequently short, straightforward sentences which contrast with the more complicated syntax of the tripartite constructions, or which are alternated with other longer, complex sentences. The total impression is of a somewhat more restrained and less flamboyant style, as dictated by the subject matter. *The Fireflies* and *In This Land* have a much increased ideological content and the emphasis is no longer on atmosphere, but on social and historical foundations and factors.

CHAPTER 6

The Short Story Collections

IN 1956, the year in which the novelist's father died, she published "Los cuentos, vagabundos"[1] ("Vagabond Stories") and *Los niños tontos*[2] *(The Stupid Children).* The latter, a collection of poematic short sketches, the first of her works devoted entirely to children and their emotional and imaginary worlds, has been one of her greatest critical successes. Matute has revealed that these little pieces were written at various odd moments; for example, while riding a bus or waiting in a café. Many were scribbled on scraps of paper, subway tickets, napkins, old envelopes, the backs of menus, and later thrown in a drawer and forgotten. Presumably several of them were thus misplaced or discarded, as they were initially written with no thought of publication. There was originally no plan to collect or to integrate them, so whatever unity emerges is accidental, due to her own internal consistency and the sincerity of her interest and involvement. The various fragments were subsequently gathered together and arranged by Matute's husband, whose idea it was to publish them. She now considers *The Stupid Children* one of her most personal creations, one of those which most satisfy her and for which she feels the most affection.

During these years while finishing work on *The Dead Children*, Matute ventured into the field of children's literature, and in 1957 gave further evidence of her growing interest in childhood and adolescence with the publication of *El tiempo*[3] *(Time)*, a collection of short stories, many with youthful protagonists. As with subsequent short story collections, *Time* contains several works published previously in magazines, newspapers, and reviews before making their appearance in book form. In most cases, the original edition has not been available, but where studies published separately have been accessible for comparison, differences are few and minor. Both in terms of accessibility and definitiveness, the collected versions seem preferable.

Historias de la Artámila (Tales of Artámila), which has a much greater unity than the other collections and was apparently conceived as an organic whole, was published in 1961, as was *El arrepentido (The Repentant One)*, a rather uneven group of earlier narratives, reissued in book form. The major themes of Matute's novels appear in varying degrees in her short stories, although because of the brevity and condensation they convey an impression of even greater emphasis on childhood, adolescence, solitude, alienation, and cruelty. The proportion of lyricism and fantasy seems greater than in the longer narratives, at the same time that the short stories are often more personal and direct in their appeal to the reader's subjectivity, and the realism consequently less. While not so numerous, however, there are also examples of seemingly objective and impassive presentation in the short stories. They range from the most lyric and tender through the fantastic vein and on to apparent cruelty at the opposite extreme.

I   Los niños tontos (The Stupid Children)

Often called prose poems by the critics, the twenty-one short sketches vary in length from a paragraph to four or five pages and run the gamut from a rather easily summarized, conventional plot line to no "story" at all. All have children as their major theme, and most contain a large dose of fantasy. The "stupid children" are not so much stupid as somewhat at odds with the world around them, misunderstood, rejected, nonconforming, or unloved. Often they are victims of their own imaginations, or simply living too much in the magic world of childhood. They personify the results of the gulf between generations, caused by adult inability to enter into or comprehend the children's world. Matute shows a certain preference for children who are sick, abnormal, deformed, or otherwise isolated from more normal activities and relationships, factors which force them to live more intensely in the world of fantasy. All are handled with great tenderness by the novelist, in contrast with the general indifference or cruelty with which they meet or react. Her presentation ranges from lyric indirectness to an understated matter-of-factness, with some stories narrated in much the form that events would be perceived and incompletely understood by childish fantasy, and others in the elliptical way a child might tell them. There is no separation of fact and fantasy, no comment or interpretation by the author. Her use of extreme solitude, cruelty, violence, deformity, death, and other unkind realities, combined with the innocence and fantasy of the children, achieves at times a shocking impact.

An extremely important theme is the death of children, which is undoubtedly something the novelist finds especially moving or disturbing, as indicated by her subjective reaction to children's cemeteries, but which probably also has a significance beyond the personal. Twelve, possibly fourteen of the sketches involve the deaths of children (there are two cases where the young protagonist is gravely injured, although it is unclear whether mortally so). Usually, the deaths are due to psychological rather than physical causes, or at least the child is brought into the fatal situation for psychological reasons, suggesting that death may symbolize the loss of childhood, or that the deaths represent an instinctive or even voluntary rejection of a too-cruel world.

The prose is extremely lyrical, imaginative, with a childlike simplicity and rhythm, and frequent use of repetitions. While suggestive of children's stories—or of stories told by children—*The Stupid Children* is not intended for a juvenile audience. Its deceptive air of childishness is due to the novelist's success in fusing form and content, but the implications of the stories are far from childish.

In "La niña fea" ("The Ugly Girl"), a child rejected and called ugly by her school companions was left alone with nature until one day the soil called to her. Then they placed paper flowers in her mouth, and everyone said, "How pretty she is." (The custom of putting paper flowers in the mouth of a dead child is peculiar to the area of Castile where Matute spent her summers as a child, and is the only textual indication of geographic locale in *The Stupid Children*. The novelist has stated, however, that "la Artámila," or Mansilla de la Sierra is the location for this collection.)

In "Polvo de carbón" ("Coal Dust"). a coal vendor's child was obsessed by the black dust filtering everywhere. Getting up one night she noticed the moonlight reflected in a large tub and presumably drowned when she tried to wash herself in the bottom of the tub. This association of the moon with the death of a child recalls García Lorca, one of Matute's favorite authors during her own childhood, and the most likely source (if there is one), despite frequency of the theme in international folklore.

"El niño que era amigo del demonio" ("The Boy Who Was the Devil's Friend") describes a little boy who felt sorry for the outcast demon, hated by everyone. While the child thinks that in return the devil will not tempt him, the sketch is a very lyric capturing of the childish potential for tenderness. "El año que no llegó" ("The Year that Never Came") relates the death of a child, a little boy about to complete his first year, but who mysteriously died instead. No cause is

even suggested, aside from the child's awareness that he is about to have
a birthday, a precocious appreciation of the passing of time.

"El negrito de los ojos azules" ("The Little Blue-Eyed Negro"),
considered retarded at birth because he did not cry, was left alone in a
basket where a cat who hated him removed his eyes. One day the child
went out the window with a sweet breeze and, discovering nature,
realized how he needed his blue eyes and sat down to wait. Gypsies
came with a trained bear who, instead of dancing, wept for the child
until he was dragged away. Leaves fell, symbolizing passage of time.
The child next inquired of a stray dog for his eyes, but the dog only
licked his face and wept. The following dawn, after the child's death,
the dog hid him in the earth, and with spring two blue flowers
appeared. Numerous elements recall Hans Christian Andersen: The
structure, with its several stages of search, the special role of animals,
the sentimentality, and the symbolic compensation through nature at
the end.

"El hijo de la lavandera" ("The Laundress's Son"), misshapen but
loved and protected by his mother, suffered from the cruelty of the
foreman's children, who made fun of his too-thin legs and too-large
head. Finally one day, throwing rocks from ambush, they split open his
deformed, bald "pumpkin head" right where his mother had kissed
him. The undisguised cruelty of the style corresponds to the spontaneous, apparently unmotivated cruelty of the other children, a
frequent Matute theme. Intensely lyric in concentration but untranslatable, a few lines recalling children's songs, rhymes, or taunts offer
variations of teasing or insulting descriptions of the child's abnormal
head, innocent and infinitely cruel.

"El árbol" ("The Tree"), reflected in a window, so fascinated a little
boy that he could think of nothing else. Obsessed, unable to sleep, he
expected the tree to come for him, until the night at last whisked the
child away among the branches of the tree. Frequently, a child's
obsession with a fantastic or imaginary thing leads to death, presented
as the eventual attainment of the elusive, fascinating object. "El
incendio" ("The Fire") also deals with the destructive power of
fantasy: a child who drew a fire with his crayons was burned to death.

The longest story of this collection, "El niño que encontró un violín
en el granero" ("The Boy Who Found a Violin in the Granary"), not
only recalls some of the unpublished juvenilia, but seems to contain
germs of two later works: "La razón" ("Reason") in *Tres y un sueño
(Thee Fantasies and a Dream)* and the children's story, "El saltamontes
verde" ("The Grasshopper"). Zum-Zum, one of many children, was

neglected because he never spoke. Too big to play and too small to work, he went one afternoon to the granary where he found an ancient violin, a dog, and a crow. The dog informed him that the violin had lost its voice at Zum-Zum's birth and warned him not to repair it, but the boy persisted. He took the violin to his oldest brother, and its shrill music was identified as the voice of Zum-Zum, who fell to the ground like a broken doll and was abandoned. The dog then came and carried him far away, a conclusion which recalls "The Little Blue-Eyed Negro" and the search for his eyes, also leading to death, wherein the child is attended by a dog. The search for missing voice and eyes is repeated by Matute in other fantastic tales or children's stories, and while obviously representing speech and sight, these must also symbolize understanding and maturation, which she often associates with death. It should be noted that in Matute's work the child may "die" (i.e., cease to be a child) as a result of growing up.

The fantastic vein is abandoned for social undercurrent and a note of satire in "El escaparate de la pastelería" ("The Pastry Shop Window"). An extremely poor child dreamed nightly of entering the window until late one night, feverish and somnambulant, he visited it to find it closed, cold, and silent. A charitable lady who came the next day with a measure of chickpeas was scandalized to hear he was not hungry. Even after disillusionment, childhood's dreams are not for sale. "El otro niño" ("The Other Boy") likewise minimizes the fantastic, while showing that the marvelous may still be found in the most prosaic places. "The Other Boy," different because he gave no evidence of fear, dreams, or questions, appeared one day in the village school where the teacher noticed that the fingers of his right hand were formed together. She knelt before him, weeping, in the belief that "The Child of the Altar has come to my school." Indirectly, this sketch suggests the normalcy of fear, fantasy, and curiosity, as the child without them appears supernatural. "La niña que no estaba en ninguna parte" ("The Little Girl Who Was Nowhere") describes the room, the clothes, the doll which once belonged to a little girl who had not died but was nowhere. Beneath the mystery and air of vague, all-prevading sorrow, Matute conceals the tragedy of growing up, the passing of a point of no return at the edge of Never-Never Land.

"El tiovivo" ("The Merry-Go-Round"), repeats the theme of a child's death as the only means of attaining the unattainable, of preserving illusion forever. One rainy day, a penniless child came to buy his ticket with a beer-bottle cap, and even though the merry-go-round was closed and silent, rode on it. In the morning, when the canvas was lifted, people fled screaming and no one rode that merry-go-round again. Death is a possibility, but not unequivocally clear in "El niño del cazador" ("The Hunter's Son"). Accustomed to accompany his father daily on the hunt and carry the game, one night the child stole the gun and went hunting on his own, "bagging fear, cold, darkness, and frost the color of blood." The hazards of growing up, including the risk of death, are increased by the child's impatience.

Two stories which deal with aspects of cruelty, one with the unconscious, instinctive cruelty of children, and the second with the child's sensitivity which converts normal events of the adult world into emotional torture, are "El niño que no sabía jugar" ("The Child Who Didn't Know How to Play") and "El corderito pascual" ("The Easter Lamb"). The little boy who didn't know how to play was not attracted by toys, which pleased his father as a sign of intelligence. But one day his mother discovered that his pastime was torturing, killing, and dismembering crickets, worms, tadpoles, and other small creatures. The latter story, by contrast, deals with a child's love for animals, a theme found in a longer story of *Time*; a fat, friendless child who receives a lamb as a pet. On Easter Sunday, moved by a horrible foreboding, the boy dashes to the kitchen to find the severed head of his only friend.

Another presentation of the death theme occurs in "La sed y el niño" ("Thirst and the Child"), wherein a little boy came every afternoon to drink at a fountain, until one day the fountain was taken away. Still he came each day, "until he was only thirst and ashes, scattered by the wind." In an ending which again recalls some of Andersen's tales, "water sprang from the earth where the fountain had been, and the voice of the stupid child, asking who had taken away his fountain, was heard every afternoon, crossing the dry land, reaching to the ocean." This is a variation of the theme of sacrifice, as the child's death buys the rebirth of the fountain, but also parallels many of Matute's tales of obsessive illusion, wherein the attainment of the desire brings death.

By contrast, "El niño al que se le murió el amigo" ("The Boy Whose Friend Died") is fairly realistic and direct. Having come to understand the meaning of death after the loss of his friend, this boy loses interest in games. When he returns home, his mother is startled to notice how he has grown and buys him a pair of long pants. Here the child neither dies nor disappears in the physical sense, although the disappearance of childhood is symbolized by the acquisition of adult garb. The awareness of the boy whose friend died is the missing ingredient in "El jorobado" ("The Hunchback"); the deformed child's lack of perception makes this one of the most pathetic pieces of the collection. The little hunchback is saddened because his father, operator of a carnival sideshow, conceals him instead of making him an object of amusement. "El niño de los hornos" ("The Child With the Ovens") is a chilling sketch of sibling rivalry. Because of the new baby, the family ignored the little boy who made mud ovens, so one night he fired the oven up and put the "skinned rabbit" of a new brother inside. Still another variation of the theme of the death of a child is seen in "Mar" ("Sea"), which closes the collection. Sent to the seashore for his health, the little boy wanted to see how deep the ocean was. He walked steadily further, finding it beautiful, but those on shore began to weep and lament. The association of the ocean with death is an ancient literary convention, utilized by Matute to dramatize the initial lack of fear and negative associations, the simple curiosity with which the small child regards death.

The literary impact of this little book belies its size and simplicity. Matute's contemporary and colleague, the Spanish novelist Camilo José Cela, considers *The Stupid Children* "The most important work written in Spanish by a woman since the Countess Emilia Pardo Bazán." Whether or not the comparison is appropriate, it calls attention to a major stylistic force and to the appearance on the Spanish literary scene of an uncommon phenomenon. Works of fantasy in Spain are extremely rare, and Matute's artistic use of fantasy in a work which must be taken seriously by adults marks the reaching of an opposite literary pole from Pardo Bazán's naturalism.

II El tiempo (Time)

Some thirteen of the novelist's earlier writings, covering a variety of subjects and ranging over several years, are grouped together under the title *Time*. The first and longest story, from which the collection takes its name, has also been published separately as a novelette, with the title *La pequeña vida*[4] *(The Small Life)*. Except for the change in title, the two versions are substantially the same. Their basic theme is solitude and the search for communication and understanding, with the implication that these, if attained at all, may be found too late.

Two orphaned adolescents, Pedro and Paulina, led a difficult existence in a fishing village, finding their only contact with human warmth and sympathy in their friendship, which was restricted by the girl's disapproving aunts. Desperately, they decided to run away and start a new life together; Paulina wore the ballet slippers inherited from her mother, her only keepsake and the symbol of her dreams. One shoe became wedged in the railroad track as they heard the whistle of the oncoming train. Unable to free Paulina, Pedro embraced her and the train ran over them both in the fog.

"La ronda" ("The Round"), also fairly lengthy, is one of Matute's better short stories, and presents a variation on the Cain theme, using friends who were once like brothers. The title refers to a round of drinks or to a night of merry-making, in this case a farewell binge for three boys leaving for the war, but it is ironic in its inapplicability to the main events. One of the conscripts, Miguel, previously not introspective and something of a bully, was filled with forebodings touched off by the sinister lamp swinging overhead, and spent the night in an effort to understand and justify his existence. Leaving home, not for the party but in search of answers, Miguel met Victor, the schoolmaster's son, formerly preoccupied with the unanswerable questions suddenly plaguing Miguel. Unaware that Victor hates him for his torments in childhood, Miguel allows himself to be lured to a lonely mountain where he is stabbed and left to die, while Victor lets everyone believe that Miguel has deserted. The dawning philosophical concern is almost directly responsible for Miguel's death, suggesting (as does the previous narrative) the difficulties and dangers inherent in changing a basic pattern of life.

In "Los niños buenos" ("The Good Children"), the eight-year-old narrator has been expelled from her *colegio* for excessive candor and sent as punishment to live with her grandfather. As she has no love either for him or the rural life, she leads the villagers to believe she is badly clothed and fed, allowed to go to indecent movies, and encouraged to steal, so that her father is summoned to take her home. Having learned the art of deception, she is now considered good by everyone but herself. The novelist has mentioned a certain autobiographical content in this story, not in the actual plot material, but in setting (Mansilla) and the fact that she, at a similar age, lived for a time with her grandparents while recuperating from an illness. The schoolmaster and some of the other villagers had real-life models.

A little orphan girl of about the same age lives with her grandfather in "Fausto," the proceeds of his organgrinding barely sufficing to maintain them in abject poverty. After the child adopted a sick, ugly cat (Fausto), her grandfather insisted she get rid of it since it could not find its own food. Unable to teach Fausto to fend for himself, the little girl killed him by cracking his head on the pavement. The parallel between the infirmities and helplessness of the grandfather and Fausto is underscored when the child explains how she killed Fausto because he was good for nothing, adding innocently, "Grandfather, I bet you're going to die soon." This may be another example of the spontaneous or unconscious cruelty of children, but there is also a distinct possibility that the remark is deliberate, a form of retribution for the sacrifice of Fausto, or even a threat.

"El amigo" ("The Friend"), a longer and more detailed version of the tale of the sacrificed Easter lamb in *The Stupid Children*, is probably artistically inferior, being less lyrical and more senti-mentalized. The social element plays a larger role, but the possible satiric intent is basically at variance with the lonely child's personal tragedy. Loneliness is a basic theme in "La frontera del pan" ("The Bread Barrier"), where communication is blocked. Enrique Babel, a discontented, envious young introvert pitied a miserable girl selling bread when he saw her mistreated by the other vendors. The girl misunderstood his attempt to help and smashed his dawning dreams by insisting on selling her bread, so that he withdrew even more deeply into himself. Another type of problem in communication is presented in "Chimenea" ("Chimney"). The form, a letter of confession is not frequently used by Matute, but resembles the device of the diary employed in *The Abel Family*. The confession is written by a drunken chimney sweep to the village priest, relating his life as the illegitimate child of a servant, orphaned at twelve, and explaining how he gave up eating and turned to drink after hearing in a sermon that it was sinful "to live for bread alone." Confession, interrupted by lengthy retro-spective reconstruction, is a technique also employed in *Celebration in the Northwest*.

One of the strangest narratives of the collection is "No hacer nada" ("Doing Nothing"). Lazy, dreamy Martin Dusco slowly let the lands go to waste, giving away crops to avoid the work of harvest, until his starving mother begged him to go hunting. Disgusted by the conversa-tion of a city hunter he met, Martin ran into the forest and threw himself down. Doing absolutely nothing, he realized how difficult and meaningless life was, and renounced the struggle. After ten days in which he moved only to drink from the stream, he finally lost consciousness and died. Something quite different is "Vida nueva" ("New Life"), in which two old men who actually have almost nothing to live for, continue to invent illusions to keep themselves alive, pretending to each other that they are happy, loved, and self-sufficient. One then goes to his boardinghouse and writes himself a New Year's card, while the other, relegated to the attic by his children, gave himself once again the last Christmas gift of his late wife.

In "Sombras" ("Shadows") the five survivors of a larger, four-generation family group (all but annihilated in a wartime bombardment) live in continual friction in the attic of a ramshackle building in a poor neighborhood. The household—grandfather, three young-adult grandchildren, and a small nephew—depends upon seventeen-year-old Lidia as cook, house-keeper, and maid-of-all-work. Her only diversion is an occasional visit to a cheap neighborhood movie, accompanied by the young nephew. The "shadows" include memories of the past, the bombing which haunts the child, the fading photos of his parents, the images on the movie screen, and soon, the remaining members of the household. The elder brother is imprisoned for fraud and vanishes after his release; the younger marries an older woman for money and also disappears from the scene. One night Lidia and her nephew return to find the grandfather's rocker before an open window, with rain drenching his dead body. Helpless, almost certainly facing separation and the loss of their home, Lidia and the child are threatened with becoming shadows, too.

"El chico de al lado" ("The Boy Next Door") is written in the form of a memoir by an adolescent girl, who adored the aloof boy next door until she met a friend of her older brother, and suddenly the neighbor seemed just a child. "Mentiras" ("Lies") were embellishments of reality invented by a one-legged harbor guard. A favorite fantasy of launching a boat of his own enabled him to begin a friendship with a poor girl who worked in a store, but this eventually forced him to carry out the project, launching a strange contraption which crashed against the seawall and caused him fatal injuries. "Los cuentos, vagabundos" ("Vagabond Stories") is not really a story, but offers the elaboration of a theory as to how a limited number of folk tales have spread throughout the world in almost infinite variation, changing only their outer dress in different countries.

Most of the stories are not especially noteworthy for their style, and because of the differing dates of composition and the variety of content, it is not meaningful to talk of style in the collection as a whole. Time, as the title suggests, is a major theme in Matute's writing, but it is more often implicit in these stories than explicit. Death, murder, the discovery or mastery of deception, cruelty, disillusionment, various emotional or external tragedies, and a change of affections provide the plot material, making it clear that the aspect of time which predominates is villainous: time the killer, the destroyer, the deceiver, and disillusioner. Time's inexorable march also brings healing, but that aspect is neglected for the most part. If a conclusion were to be based on *Time*, it would be that with Time, one always loses more than is gained.

III   Historias de la Artámila[5] (Tales of Artámila)

The thematic unity of *Tales of Artámila* is slightly less than in *The Stupid Children* but considerably stronger and more easily perceptible than in *Time*. The twenty-two stories range from a minimum of three to a maximum of ten pages. While all share a common setting—the mountain village of Matute's childhood summers in Old Castile—some portray social or economic problems of the villagers and peasants; others describe an illusion or its loss, an awakening, an injustice, or a secret sentiment. The general tone is melancholic, in keeping with the somber background, and many of the stories either end in tragedy or present a situation tragic in itself. A classic theme of Spanish literature, the incompatibility of illusion and reality, is crucial in many of the *historias*.

"El incendio" ("The Fire") has no common content with the sketch of the same name in *The Stupid Children*, and no connection between the two is immediately apparent. It is more likely an unconscious duplication of title, but it is possible that fire has some consistent symbolic significance in Matute's work. In that event, *incendio* would be closely linked with the destructive force, both tangible and intangible, of illusion. "The Fire" concerns the sickly son of a drunken schoolmaster in a horribly poor, grim, brutal village. Illusion entered his life for the first time on his sixteenth birthday, when the village was visited by a company of traveling actors. At a dance after the performance, he was dazzled by an actress who later let him make love to her in a wheatfield. To prevent her departure with the troupe, he burned their wagons, but then in the light of dawn saw her clearly, disheveled, vulgar, much older than he thought. Disillusioned, he confessed to her and waited while she denounced him to the police. The strolling players, a frequent Matute motif, are here seen in their role of bringing illusion, dreams, and a chance of escape to the isolated, miserable villages, as is likewise found in "Envidia" ("Envy"). Illusion, however, is frequently paired with its opposite, and thus the vagabond actors may also bring deception, disappointment, and disillusionment as happens in "The Fire" and in the novelette, *Celebration in the Northwest.*

Illusion also plays a vital role in "Don Payasito" ("Mr. Clown"), related from a point of view within the fantasy world of children. This story contains a certain amount of autobiographical material, literarily transformed; it is based on an experience of the novelist and the brother closest to her in age, but most of the details have been changed. Two children frequently visited old Lucas, who read their palms, told them stories, and could summon "Don Payasito" to entertain them. One day they found Lucas dead, but were only mildly upset until finding in his old trunk the costume of Don Payasito; they then began to cry disconsolately. The importance of illusion is likewise emphasized in "La felicidad" ("Happiness"), wherein it becomes a life-sustaining barrier against a cruel reality. A new rural doctor, arriving late at night, was told there was nowhere to stay in the village except the home of a woman who was crazy, although clean and harmless. He was favorably impressed by the pleasant woman and given the room of her son, who was in the city. Having decided to continue rooming with her, he was informed by a village official that the woman had no son; the boy had died over four years before. That shadowy zone where illusion and psychosis merge, where a "normal" fantasy ceases to be normal, is one of the novelist's special interests.

"Pecado de omisión" ("Sin of Omission") presents another form of reacting to the encounter with a too-harsh reality. The wealthy village mayor took in an orphaned distant relative, but instead of educating the obviously intelligent boy, sent him to the mountains as a shepherd, where the difficult, primitive life and isolation reduced him to semi-animalism. Much later, when a visit to the village brought him face to face with differences between himself and former friends, the boy kills his "benefactor" with a rock. Another case of violence in the young, closely related to the effects of illusion, is found in "The River." Here illusion has not been destroyed, but functions as the destroyer. The boy drowned himself believing he had killed the schoolmaster by poisoning his wine with river flowers which childish lore held to be lethal. Actually, the man died of pneumonia.

"Los alambradores" ("The Metalworkers"), "La chusma" ("The Rabble") and "Los chicos" ("The Boys") illustrate various facets of the Castilian villagers' intense localism which manifests itself most frequently in intolerance or hostility to outsiders, carried at times to unreasoning extremes as will be seen in "El Mundelo" ("Mundelo"). In "The Metalworkers," an old man and his grandson abandon a company of vagabond actors for the relative stability of the village, hoping to support themselves honorably as metalworkers. However, most village residents refuse either to give them work or to sell them food on credit, insisting that they are untrustworthy. They consider their suspicions justified when the child is starved into stealing, and the would-be metalworkers are run out of town. This aspect of village psychology may at times be counterbalanced by acts of generosity, but such acts of charity are usually reserved for the "natives." The novelist was obviously impressed by this narrowness of the village mentality when she made it the theme of several works. "La chusma" is the label applied to the miners, most of whom have been brought from afar and are forced to live in segregation, thus perpetuating separation from the village. One extremely poor mining family bought the largest codfish available for Christmas (a symbol of luxury and status among the villagers), but then ironically saw the father near death when a bone stuck in his throat. The alcoholic doctor summoned to treat him refused to remove the bone until the family had collected 200 pesetas owed on a previous bill, and later laughed about the patient's choking. The figure of the brutalized and alcoholic doctor (found in *The Abel Family* and elsewhere) corresponds to similar portrayals of the schoolmaster, insofar as both represent the educated type of superior culture or sensitivity which cannot survive in the village environment.

"The Boys" has a large autobiographical content and has been discussed in connection with Matute's childhood when, as a little girl, she witnessed the brutal beating administered by a much larger boy to a child from one of the despised families of the prison camp. This seems to have been the moment of her first awareness of social injustice, and the experience has acquired a thoroughly symbolic value for her. At the same time, she became aware of how much children have in common, regardless of class or background, that "a child is a child," even when life has forced him prematurely into other patterns of action. The solitude of the childish victim is mutely, graphically portrayed, and further underlined by the young narrator's failure to communicate her sympathy. A similar desperate solitude is shown in "El Mundelo," a miner without a family, an outsider suffering from an occupational lung disease. His work is apparently his only "possession," and the fear of losing it becomes such that the normally passive Mundelo knifes a man who taunts him for his illness. A secondary theme has to do with that desperate isolation wherein even an unpleasant relationship is preferable to complete loneliness; thus Mundelo lives only to return to the village which always spurned him, but where at least the faces were familiar. En route to prison when his train was wrecked, Mundelo did not attempt to escape, but helped to save others, thinking thereby to appease village opinion. Having served his sentence, he returned "home" but was stoned out of town, despite the townspeople's knowledge of his heroism. The powerful attraction of even a negative sentiment when compared with nothingness, the absence of any personal contact, is repeatedly treated by Matute.

The reverse situation is less common in her writings, but also occurs, as in "Caminos" ("Roads"), when a boy sacrifices the one true emotional tie of his life in a silent act of gratitude. A childless old couple whose only treasure was a horse, Crisántemo, one day took in the wounded, abused child of gypsies who had abandoned him when he was unable to travel further. "Barrito" ("Dusty"), treated as a son, was always obedient, but seemed to feel no love for his benefactors. Four years later, the boy's failing sight required an operation which could only be paid for by selling Crisántemo. When Barrito learned of the impending sale, he disappeared rather than permit them to make this sacrifice for him, choosing the hard life of the roads he had known before, and probably inevitable blindness. This is another aspect of the existential motif of incommunication, the inability to communicate found in a majority of Matute characters. Here, however, silence is the result of inexpressible love and gratitude which cannot be reduced to words.

In "La fiesta" ("The Celebration") the novelist reiterates the importance of dreams or illusion, as well as the effects of solitude, important in so many of her stories. Eloísa, the mentally retarded daughter of an unmarried servant, orphaned at the age of twelve, was sent to the mountains as a shepherdess, much like the boy in "Sin of Omission." With the difference that Eloísa was not intelligent and she was not deprived of education, she too suffered the extremes of solitude, coming down to the village only once every three months. At the age of fifteen, Eloísa was invited to the annual village *fiesta*, and the master promised to pay for her wedding if she found a sweetheart. The *fiesta* became an overpowering illusion in her life previously devoid of dreams, but Eloísa had to work so hard the day before that she slept through the entire festivities. Numbed, uncomprehending, apparently unable to adjust to waiting another year, she was found two days later in the mountains, dead. An entirely different sort of illusion is destroyed in "El gran vacío" ("The Great Void"). A patient, kind old man was hatefully abused by his invalid wife, to the point that the neighborhood children came to wish for her death, imagining that this would allow him a chance at happiness. But when the harping wife died, he closed his house and left the village, seeking admittance to an asylum for the aged, reiterating the novelist's view that an unhappy relationship is better than solitude.

"Bernardino," the protagonist in the tale of the same name, was supposedly a spoiled brat, disliked by other children, and seemingly loved only by his dog, Chu, for whom he showed no overt affection. When the village boys captured Chu to torture him, however, Bernardino agreed to let them beat him instead. His stoic acceptance of suffering recalls the theme of "Roads," to the extent that, in the absence of communication, a child may choose self-sacrifice as an expression of love.

The importance of illusion, particularly in the life of the invalid child, is treated with delicate, poetic realism in "El rey" ("The King") and "La rama seca" ("The Dry Branch"). In the former of these, Dino, a paralyzed nine-year-old, lived a dull, empty life until the new schoolmaster came after hours to teach him to read, bought him books, and opened up the world of fantasy and imagination. At Christmas, the schoolmaster promised Dino a visit from one of the "Three Kings" (Spanish children's presents are brought by the Magi rather than Santa Claus), but after hearing the boy's fantasy description of the king, renounced his projected impersonation as he realized it could never compete with Dino's dream. "The Dry Branch" was the only toy and companion of a little girl sick with Maltese fever. This solitary child called her stick "Pipa" and chattered endlessly to it, until one day her older brother threw the rudimentary doll away. The little girl was disconsolate even after a neighbor bought her an expensive doll, and subsequently made a series of Pipas, each unsuccessful. The spring following the child's death, this lady found Pipa and saw that the stick-doll was indeed unique, with a melancholy beauty. While the tale itself is not in the realm of fantasy, the atmosphere recalls the powerful fantasy world of a child, as well as the frequency with which that fantasy may center upon an unlikely object, at times with unexpected or fatal results. It is frequent in Matute's treatment of children that both the attainment and the loss of these fantasy symbols may be associated with death.

The association of a fantasy-related occupation with death is found in "Los pájaros" ("The Birds"), whose child-protagonist is also isolated, not only because of a slight physical deformity, but because of his father's occupation as forest ranger. The boy, who seemed to have a mysterious facility for communicating with the birds, used to climb to the top of a tall tree to talk with them. Some time after a fatal fall from the treetop, the boy's clothes were sold to make a scarecrow, but instead, birds came in flocks. The special importance which trees have in a number of Matute stories may well be due to her own feeling for them as a child, and her habit of escaping to the river and trees from the adult world. The frequent association of the tree with the death of a child (already seen, for example, in the "The Tree" in *The Stupid Children*) is not so easily explainable, but it does usually relate to attainment of the child's dream or fantasy. Such is the case of "El árbol de oro" ("The Tree of Gold"), in which the novelist combines realism with the marvelous or supernatural. Ten-year-old Ivo claimed he could see a tree of gold through a crack in the crumbling wall of a locked room in the ancient village school, but when the narrator was able to look, she saw only barren earth. Returning to the area two years later, she passed the cemetery at sunset and saw a tree of gold, and beneath it, a small cross with Ivo's name.

A more common kind of gold appears in "El tesoro" ("The Treasure"), which illustrates the relativity of wealth. A miserably poor peasant, rumored to have found buried treasure, was severely beaten by would-be thieves. After his injuries healed, he told the woman who had nursed him he could no longer bear the responsibility of the treasure, and since she also feared accepting it, they agreed to distribute it to the poor. The "treasure" proved to be a single gold coin, implying that even material wealth is an illusion.

"La conciencia" ("Conscience") is an entirely different sort of story, suggesting that everyone has done something of which to be ashamed. Its atmosphere and structure recall the folk tale, and it has a similar purpose, for it illustrates that guilt can also create or perpetuate illusions. A mysterious vagabond succeeds in getting an innkeeper's wife to let him stay indefinitely without paying, hinting that otherwise he will reveal something he has seen. When finally, in desperation, she prefers exposure to keeping him around any longer, he tells her he has seen nothing and suggests that she keep an eye on her husband, since he, too, has put up with the vagabond's presence.

Closing the collection, "El perro perdido" ("The Lost Dog") is a tale of sympathetic magic, wherein a boy who is gravely ill saves a stray dog from torture. During the night, the boy recuperates completely while the dog becomes progressively sicker and weaker. The dog dies at dawn, and the boy insists that the dog has saved him, giving him his health. This is a theme found in a number of folk and fairy tales, and has been used by Matute elsewhere with slight variations. Here there may very likely be an influence of Hans Christian Andersen, possibly no longer conscious on the novelist's part.

Tales of Artámila has received relatively little critical attention as an individual entity,[6] and while it is not comparable to her major novels, it is worthy of more detailed study. The attention given to the area of "la Artámila" (setting of *Celebration in the Northwest, The Dead Children, The River,* presumably of the final part of *The Fireflies,* and of *The Abel Family* as well as—according to the novelist—of *The Stupid Children),* suggests that the importance of these tales is greater than their proportionate size. Knowing that the place and conditions described have a real-life referent contributes to appreciation of the social and economic problems inspiring or underlying many of the *historias.* At the same time, the recurrence of many of Matute's obsessive themes in this collection makes it one of her most "typical" and an excellent introduction for those not familiar with her writing.

IV   El arrepentido ("The Repentant One")

The stories collected beneath this title[7] have no immediately evident unifying theme or setting as was the case with *Time* and *Tales of Artámila.* Unlike the stories of *Time, The Repentant One* seems not to have the former's linking motifs and recurrent concerns. If there is a common theme suggested by the title, it must be that all the characters have something to regret, for most of the events related are regrettable in one or more aspects. However, repentance is not applicable in many cases, for the unhappy situation or outcome does not always result from an error of the protagonist, but from factors beyond his or her control, often social or economic. With one or two exceptions, there is a pronounced social implication, or strongly suggested social criticism. Even in those stories where fantasy seemingly predominates, poverty is an important factor, looming in the background. Two other stories in the collection deal rather directly with the Spanish Civil War, which suggests that the selective criteria applied in gathering these stories together may be similar to the creative impulse which inspires an overwhelming percentage of Matute's work of the past decade, an obsessive preoccupation with the social and economic factors underlying the physical and psychological violence of Spain's civil conflict.

In the title story, the repentant person is old Tomeu, an aging tavernkeeper and one-time smuggler who has raised his nephew, Ruti, and financed his medical studies. No specific location is mentioned, but an island is indicated, and dialectical forms and names point to one of the Balearic Islands. Shortly after Ruti's graduation, old Tomeu requests a physical examination and is informed that he has only a month or two to live. He implies that he will make his nephew his heir, and while the young man avoids discussing the "painful" topic, he does not decline the inheritance. Tomeu commits suicide three days later, and Ruti receives a letter indicating that his uncle was well aware there was nothing wrong with his health, but that his nephew wished to drive him to suicide. The examination situation was a test which Ruti failed. Tired of living, and having ascertained the unworthiness of his heir apparent, Tomeu left his smuggling fortune to an orphanage in a surprise ending of the sort not too frequent in Matute, although other examples can be found. This particular story is an admirable example of narrative economy and concentration, and its style is much more stark and unadorned than the "typical" Matute narrative. The "surprise" ending, which has been compared with O'Henry's technique, is found in several tales of this collection.

"La luna" ("The Moon") is part of that fantastic vein frequently uncovered in the novelist's juvenilia. Here, as previously, the moon is associated with the loss or death of a child, but "Botitas" ("Bootsie") differs from most of Matute's small protagonists in that he is never neglected or cruelly treated. Quite the contrary: his parents seem to live only for him, and consider no request too extravagant, no sacrifice too great, a situation unparalleled in this writer's narratives. Such uniqueness suggests a possible model or exterior influence in the legend of the king who ordered that his son's every wish be fulfilled. In fact, Botitas, like the king's son, one night asks for the moon, but unlike the legendary prince, attains his wish, ascending an endless ladder from his window through the night sky to the "boat of the Moon." The parents' desperate effort to follow on the ground ends at last in realization that Botitas will never return. While the connection is not entirely clear, the moral seems to be that the parents sinned or erred in expecting great things of their son and so feeling superior and confident about the future. The moralizing tendency recalls examples in the juvenilia, but the exact relation to more frequent tales in which the child protagonist is an orphan, neglected, abused, or misunderstood, is in need of clarifying, as both mistreatment and overindulgence seem to lead to the same conclusion.

In sharp contrast is the total realism of "Los de la tienda" ("The Ones From the Store"), whose atmosphere of grayness and misery is similar to many stories in *Tales of Artámila*. The setting, a rather desolate area near the sea, possibly one of the poorer suburbs of Barcelona, is frequently contrasted in the young protagonist's memory with the village of his childhood. Different levels of poverty are presented, the more fortunate position being occupied by twelve-year-old Dionisio, who works long hours without pay in his godfather's store. He envies the band of boys from the adjacent shantytown, relatively free, but desperately hungry. Neither they nor Dionisio have a childhood in the full sense (one of Matute's favorite themes, and one of the charges implicitly leveled against social injustices, which rob childhood of its magic). In his loneliness and need to be accepted, as well as out of some vague sense of guilt and desire to help, Dionisio takes the one hundred peseta bill his godfather has given him after much pleading and gives it to Manolito, leader of the gang, to buy desperately needed groceries for his family. These good intentions are subsequently misinterpreted, for the bill proves to be counterfeit, and Manolito is subject to much verbal abuse and kicked out of the godfather's store. The loneliness and helplessness of both Dionisio and Manolito in the adult world, where both have roles as victims, contrasts with the apparent total heartlessness and egotism of the godfather, whose role is that of the stereotyped merchant or moneylender, an extreme of avarice and greed.

"El hijo" ("The Son") also deals with a social and emotional injustice, hypocrisy, and false charity. Doña Catalina, a childless, wealthy *beata* (excessively religious woman), has "adopted" the illegitimate son of her unmarried servant girl and is raising him as a son or godson, having told the boy his mother died when he was born, while the real mother serves them as a maid, abused and insulted by her son, unable to express either affection or resentment. The boy is extremely egotistical, clever at worming money out of his "godmother," but otherwise apparently indifferent to her. Matute is fond of exposing deviations from true Christian charity, which she usually does indirectly, showing how certain emotional satisfactions are exacted (but not acknowledged) under the guise of purely religious motivation, generally a camouflage for egotism or some other base or perverse passion. As one astute commentator of this story has observed, "the religious content is used to expose pharisaism by ironic contrast."[8] The narrative technique employed is especially interesting, as the novelist creates a counterpoint between the reflections of the maid, which reveal the extremes of cruelty or insensitivity to which her maternal feelings have been subjected in the name of charity, and the ritual recitation of the Joys of Mary on the rosary, led every day at dusk by Doña Catalina. A secondary counterpoint is set up between the complaints of the obese "godmother" about her heart and the heartaches of the mother who for sixteen years has been denied all expression of affection for her son. The futility of any attempt at bridging the gap is ironically underlined when the son arrives, discovers Doña Catalina dead of a heart attack, and announces her death to the maid in vulgar slang and with offhand indifference. In this case, that false charity so repugnant to the novelist would seem to have received its just deserts.

"Navidad para Carnavalito" ("Christmas for Carnavalito") brings together several Matute motifs: the orphan, the death of a child, the mountebanks or traveling players, the circus, and the attraction of these for the child. A little orphan boy, Carnavalito, either recalls or has invented a past with itinerant entertainers who took him from village to village with their tambourines and dancing bear. He entertains other children in the orphanage with his disguises and inventions, and lives only for the promised Christmas visit to the circus, which does not materialize for him because he is sick with pneumonia. Feverish, Carnavalito escapes on Christmas Eve in search of the circus and the clowns he believes to be his parents, only to be found the following dawn, frozen stiff and white. A symbolic attainment in fantasy of his goal, the sound of clowns and drums, coincides with his death, recalling a number of similar scenes in *The Stupid Children*. The ironic association of Christmas with tragedy or the death of a child is found in a number of Matute's stories (e.g., "Sino espada" ["Rather, a Sword"], which closes this collection), and may be an unconscious carry-over from childhood perusals of Hans Christian Andersen ("The Little Match Girl," for example) or a deliberate artistic juxtaposition of opposites— life-death, joy-grief, etc.—which is frequent in her work.

The title of "El hermoso amanecer" ("The Beautiful Dawn") is fiercely ironic when contrasted with the situation portrayed by the novelist. In the coldest part of winter, a last-ditch defense of a small Republican stronghold, perhaps one of the suburbs of Barcelona, is undertaken by a dozen men and a woman, who has with her her ten-year-old son, Remo. The nameless woman and mother, dressed like a man in militia garb with a military haircut, is a most uncommon female figure in Matute's writing. In the heat of battle, when the trench is soaked with blood and only his mother and two men remain alive, Remo runs away, unwilling to stay there and die. Looking back at a shout, he sees his mother aiming at him and throws himself down in time to hear the shot pass above his head. Subsequently reaching the comparative safety of a ruined shack, he sees his mother and the two men executed by the Nationalist soldiers, then lies on the ground remembering his father's letters and the jumbled, idealistic phrases of the Socialists' dreams until he is found and dragged forth by the triumphant enemy. No names or identifying labels are used for either side, but the situation makes any mistake in identification almost impossible. Matute's obsessive interest in the defense and fall of Barcelona—seen in *The Fireflies/In This Land*, in *The Dead Children*, and in *Los soldados lloran de noche (The Soldiers Weep at Night)*—the time of year, and the reference to the outskirts of a city will suggest that this is yet another vision of those closing minutes of the war when Barcelona was finally taken by Franco. This would give a special interest to "The Beautiful Dawn" within the context of the novelist's portrayals of the fall of Barcelona, since it has previously been shown through the eyes of noncombatants, or intellectuals sympathetic to the Republican cause, not from the viewpoint of working-class members of the People's Militia, determined to die in the wreckage of their dreams. It is probably for this reason that Matute is careful to omit geographic clues, names, and other specific, controversial details. The assumption is that the novelist has exercised "self-censorship" in advance, although the possibility also exists that more concrete details were eliminated by the censors.

"El campo de algodón" ("The Cotton Field") offers additional evidence of the novelist's interest in children and solitude, particularly the solitude of abnormal children. "Taquito" is an orphan and a cripple, two factors which redouble his solitude, and has recently been separated both from the setting of his childhood and his only friend, a shoemaker who was teaching him the trade. There are suggestions that he was an illegitimate child, and that his mother, long dead, had syphilis. The death of the husband of one of his three aunts has made all four dependent on a rich relative who owns a cotton field, and employs the three women, leaving the boy alone with his awareness that he is a burden. The cause of his death is not clear, as it is related indirectly, interspersed with a fantastic vision of destruction of the cotton field by wind and water, but Taquito had in his hand a sharp awl, and a fall is involved. Whether accident or suicide, his death is obviously due to loneliness and neglect, and the subsequent real-life destruction of the cotton crop is made to seem his personal vengeance, present in the power of the wind and the water envisioned as he died. More clearly than in many of the novelist's relatively realistic works, this mixture of realism and fantasy shows Taquito to be a victim of a complex of social problems, from those surrounding his birth through those embodied in the prejudice with which society at times treats the abnormal individual, or its neglect of the orphan, to the sentiments of isolation and futility which underlie his death.

"El salvamento" ("The Rescue") has a title which like many in this collection, is ironic. Timoteo, a painfully shy and relatively unattractive adolescent, is one of three boys employed for the summer by the owner of a small restaurant on the beach. The two larger boys tease and torment Timoteo endlessly, even more cruelly after discovering his love for Margarita, the employer's daughter. Late one afternoon, the three contrived a plan to force Timoteo, who never swam, into the water, by having Margarita pretend to drown. Just as they had planned, Timoteo dashed into the water to rescue Margarita, and as he sank from sight the others realized he did not know how to swim. Perhaps the most prominent theme here is that of cruelty, which Matute often treats as natural or spontaneous in children (still insufficiently subjected to the civilizing acculturation process), and which survives in lesser degree in the adolescent, to reappear sporadically and arbitrarily in adult life. Inherent cruelty in the young is a favorite theme with many postwar Spanish writers, notably Camilo José Cela and Juan Goytisolo in addition to Matute, and has been seen as an attempt to explain the brutality of the Civil War, experienced by these writers while themselves at an impressionable age.

"La señorita Bibiana" ("Miss Vivian") is difficult to fit into Matute's total production, both because the protagonist is not a common figure in her writing (Miss Vivian is a romantic, old maid schoolteacher), and because it contains a degree of sentimentalism rare in the novelist even when dealing with children, whom she normally treats with greater tenderness than she does adults, albeit usually without sentimentality. The style is not typical of the mature Matute, and a certain superficiality in characterization recalls her juvenilia, suggesting that the composition of this story antedates most of the others in *The Repentant One*, although there seem to have been some corrections made with respect to the version published in the earlier collection.[9] Thematically, "Miss Vivian" has little or nothing in common with the other narratives grouped under the collection's title. After the death of her mother, Miss Vivian begins to decline physically, to be even more melancholy and sour than before, and shortly after, to notice strange, inexplicable happenings such as changes in the grades she has given her pupils, and mysterious messages directed to her on the school blackboard. She refuses to see the doctor, believing she detests him, until at last he is summoned by her servant and diagnoses the case as somnambulism. It seems that during her sleepwalking, Miss Vivian expresses her true feelings, including a repressed romantic attachment to the doctor, and while asleep attempts to "rouse" her waking self to capture life's opportunities before it is too late.

"El maestro" ("The Schoolmaster"), one of the longest narratives in the collection, is also one of the most significant. Both the title and the placing immediately afterwards in the text may suggest a thematic relationship with "Miss Vivian," but aside from the rather superficial coincidence of professions (which are presented in very different lights), there is none. There are many similarities, however, between this story and the long section in *The Fireflies/In This Land*, which treats Pablo's career as a village schoolmaster. In both cases, the poverty and ignorance of the villages have an evident causal relationship to the involvement of the two masters in revolutionary violence at the outbreak of the Civil War. Both schoolmasters are variations of a Matute archetype, the village teacher first encountered by her in Mansilla de la Sierra, embittered by the poverty, brutalized, and driven to alcoholism by the ignorance around him and his own isolation.

Many typical Matute themes and motifs can be identified in "The Schoolmaster," a particularly representative piece appropriate for inclusion in anthologies or for study as an introduction to the writer. The isolated village with its empty, crumbling ducal palace, symbol of absentee landlordism and a decadent, unproductive aristocracy, is reminiscent of similar unequal concentrations of wealth in the hands of one family as portrayed in *The Abel Family, The Dead Children, Celebration in the Northwest*, and several short stories. The master has been over twenty years in the village, has long since quit wearing the tie he wore in the beginning for Sunday mass, frequently goes without shoes, and long ago lost his illusions of doing some good for humanity. He no longer reads newspapers, has lost his one-time interest in politics, and begins and ends his day in the bar. Considered crazy by the villagers, he is mocked by the children and does not respect himself. His sudden revolutionary fury, like that of most of the villagers, has little ideological content and is more than anything an outburst against self and circumstances. Matute has shown repeated interest in what might be called the psychology of the revolutionary, and almost always the causes portrayed are more personal than social, though social circumstances make even more difficult the self-realization of already handicapped individuals.

Despite his initial sympathy with the revolution, the emotional outburst against his life of hunger, poverty, humiliation, and injustice which leads to joining the illiterate local rebels, the master is unable to become one of the revolutionaries psychologically. He relives his youth, recalling how he was "sold" to the wealthy, alcoholic old lady who passed as his godmother and made of him a sexual plaything in return for paying his tuition. The breaking point with the rebel band is reached suddenly, irrationally, when he refuses to permit their destruction of a larger-than-life painting in the ducal palace, a painting which has fascinated him for years, becoming a vague symbol not completely understood by him. Apparently an allegorical representation of Christ, the painting is surprisingly, ironically, entitled "El maestro." When one of the rebels, a former student of the schoolmaster's, slashes the painting, he grabs the leader's gun and shoots first the vandal, then the rebel leader. After two days of hiding in the mountains, he observes the arrival of the counterrevolutionary troops, and descending to the village is denounced as one of the rebels. Without attempting to explain, he asks permission only to go to his room for his long-forgotten tie, which he wears in silence during the brief time remaining until executed by a firing squad.

The story is rich in implications, but the most eloquent seem to be that while the individual, personal motivations underlying manifestations of collective violence are eminently human and comprehensible, the ideological motives are minimal, and altruistic involvement is the exception rather than the rule. It is understandable, then, that Matute's plea is for very limited revolution, a sort which would respect certain basic principles: the intangible sentiment of religion, culture, symbols of human accomplishment, art, and that vague area of each individual where dignity and integrity reside. This, at least, seems to be the reason for which the unheroic hero first breaks with the revolutionaries, and for which he subsequently goes silently to his death, perhaps in self-castigation for his own weakness and desertion of the principles of culture and altruism with which he came to the village. The tie which he dons as his last act is symbolic of a more civilized self, almost forgotten, of his lost faith and church attendance, and of his status as a person of culture among the rude peasants. By putting it on, he reaffirms his previous break with the revolutionaries and symbolically becomes the man of twenty years ago, the young idealist who had hoped to bring knowledge to the remote, backward area which destroyed him spiritually long before bringing about his doom physically. "The Schoolmaster" is essential to an understanding of the novelist's social and political thought.

The final story in this collection, "Sino espada"[10] ("Rather, a Sword"), also has a significant social content, in addition to the themes of the rebellion of the adolescent against the adult world and its values, a frequent, almost inescapable motif in Matute's treatment of the adolescent. The novelist occasionally makes effective, ironic use of biblical quotations, to underscore hypocrisy and that self-serving "false charity" which is one of her particular dislikes, the more so as it seems to be a pretext for avoiding any real progress in the eradication of inequalities and social injustice. At the same time, she implicitly criticizes "charity" because it may humiliate the receiver, or require a modification of conduct in exchange. The story contrasts the true charity of the child's humanitarian impulses, given simply and unconditionally upon recognition of need, with organized or official forms of charity available only to those who meet certain conditions and follow certain rules. There is more political content present than may be immediately evident to the casual observer. In order to understand the full implications of Matute's treatment of the "false charity" theme, it is necessary to bear in mind that the *Falange* (Phalanx, or political party supporting Franco) long recommended the practice of "charity" as an effective substitute for any social or economic reforms.

"Rather, a Sword" exemplifies the novelist's occasional use of biblical material, not necessarily from a "specifically Christian or even conventionally religious outlook,"[11] but as "artistic raw material" with a fairly universal set of symbolic and moral connotations. The title is based on the relatively little-known pronouncement of Christ, "I have come not to bring peace but a sword," and several other quotations are placed throughout the story, set off and in italics. Their applicability to specific modern contexts is ironically demonstrated by the section of the story immediately following. The biblical quotes have been selected with evident emphasis on social content or implication, for what they contain of denunciation of social injustice, of economic exploitation and inequities, (for example, Matt. 23:4), and implicit condemnation of those who accept and perpetuate such situations while giving lip service to Christian principles.

Twelve-year-old Ripo and his mother work long hours in exchange for room and board "charitably" provided by distant relatives, Don Marcelino and Doña Elpidia. As storekeepers, these two are "both literal and figurative examples of the *mercaderes*"[12] (merchants) indicated in the title of Matute's novelistic trilogy, a term which can loosely be explained as including all those who profit directly or indirectly from the misery of others. Ripo is criticized for his visits to the slum section to talk with an old shepherd from his home town. The hill above the city, beyond the cemetery, is half covered with huts and caves, inhabited by the socially unfit—maimed, retarded, old and sick, those unable to support themselves or cast off from society like Rosa, who had an illegitimate child because the father was put in jail before he could marry her, and who has had to become a prostitute to support herself and the baby. Ripo is continually warned not to allow his employer to learn of his visits there, because "Don Marcelino is very religious and wants only decent people near him."

Christmas, because of its traditional association with joy, giving, and love, is ironically employed by the novelist to underscore the gap between the true spirit of Christmas and actual practice. On that date, Ripo and el Chapo, the old shepherd, learn that Rosa has been arrested. El Chapo cannot care for her child because there is no money or food, so the two seek help from Doña Magdalena, head of the Ladies Auxiliary (a supposedly charitable organization of the church). Ignoring all human and emotional considerations, Doña Magdalena favors putting the old man and baby in institutions. Don Marcelino rejects Ripo's plea to give them shelter in his house, and both are hauled away, weeping, while Ripo is severely rebuked for his lack of manners and ordered to hurry and ready himself for church. It would be over-simplification to say that "Rather, a Sword" portrays a world where the rich are automatically good and the poor bad, but this is an approximation of the mentality of Don Marcelino, Doña Elpidia, Doña Magdalena, and even the mother of Ripo, forced by misery and desperation to accept the standards of her "benefactors." Matute makes it abundantly clear that their moral blindness or double standards are part of a permanent set of attitudes, rather than of occasional misjudgment. This is indicated by details such as the fact that Don Marcelino and Doña Elpidia magnanimously share their table but not their menu with Ripo and his mother, as the former are served partridge while the latter eat chickpeas.

This story constitutes an excellent summary of Matute's social and religious thought, and is one of the clearest statements of her subjective reaction to injustice, hypocrisy, and false charity. True charity for her is something very close to loving and believing in one's neighbor, and has little to do with the sort of "benevolence" described in "Rather, a Sword." While there is no preaching, no denunciation by either the novelist or a character serving as mouthpiece, her message is clearly implicit in events themselves. Both from the point of view of technique and of attitude, "Rather, a Sword" should be required reading on any list, however brief, for the student of Matute.

Matute's short stories cover an even wider range of subjects than her novels, and at least as long a span of time, so that any attempt to generalize about their style and content is almost automatically invalidated. They are necessarily uneven in quality, owing to chronological differences of composition, and clear progression or development cannot be established because dates of publication frequently do not correspond to the dates of writing. Nevertheless, many of the stories and even complete collections are eminently deserving of further study, particularly the thematic aspect. Any selection of them will serve as a fairly reliable introduction to the novelist, since almost all contain ideas, types, and motifs more fully developed in longer works, and a thorough acquaintance with them is obviously essential for anyone who aspires to a complete vision of the writer.

V   Algunos muchachos (A Few Kids)

Matute's latest volume of short stories appeared in the final weeks of 1968. Classified as *narraciones* (narrations), that ambiguous Spanish genre including everything from the short short story to novelette, these tales range in length from fifteen to seventy-five pages. The collection takes its title from the first and longest story, which at first glance seems but another of her many treatments of adolescence. But both in this tale and others of the collection there are new elements which make the stories especially interesting for those following Matute's evolution as a writer.

Each *narración* is preceded by a quotation (generally poetic) from Pablo Neruda or Rafael Alberti, and in one case, from Genesis. These lines offer an enigmatic commentary on the content or interpretation of the tale which follows—a technique which Matute has utilized previously, both with short stories and full-length novels, drawing most frequently on biblical sources. The book as a whole is likewise preceded by an unidentified, italicized paragraph, seemingly quoted or paraphrased, which ends with the line, "We might know them by a sign, a cipher, or a star. . . ." Those familiar with the novelist's obsessive themes and motives will probably think at once of the "mark of Cain," and Cain-Abel imagery is present, explicitly or implicitly, in each of the stories. With one exception, each story involves a crime (usually murder or arson), motivated by hate, envy, or a confused love-hate combination. In most cases, the actual crime is only suggested and not described, alluded to so briefly, vaguely, lyrically, or incompletely that only a hint or an intuition of violence is conveyed. What is more fully presented is the emotional background and climate, the motivation, often confused, rambling, or almost incoherent, but inseparable from the psychology or situation of the characters.

A refinement of the narrator's art is apparent in the pruning and paring which has taken place in most stories of this collection. Matute, always a model of economy in her selection of a few significant, characteristic details in the presentation of personalities and environments, has here eliminated intermediate stages of action so that some readers may feel less sure about *what* happened than *why* it happened. The effect is to deepen the tone of mystery which almost always accompanies Matute's evocations of childhood and adolescence. The result is more sophisticated and consequently may require a more sophisticated reader. At the same time, there has been some suppression of the novelist's personality, her strongly individualistic style, those elements which previously could be identified as most typically Matute. The new style seems at times to show a fleeting influence of Juan Rulfo, a Mexican writer with whose works she became acquainted about 1965. However, not all changes are necessarily the result of another writer's influence; the nebulous, slightly out-of-focus vision of reality presented in these stories need not reflect the similar focus of Rulfo, but could conceivably be a development of that mixture of realism and stylized fantasy which characterized *Little Theater* and subsequently all but disappeared from her work.

The title story, "A Few Kids," reveals a Matute at once familiar and different. The setting is the oft-used Castilian mountain village (Hegroz/La Artámila) with the grandmother's house, the river and forest, and the prison camp nearby. Familiar notes are struck by themes such as the separation between the worlds of children and adults, the passing of time, the excitement and pain of the essentially solitary experience of growing up. The reader is also very much aware of another Matute constant, social inequity, subliminally emphasized, and its role in the origins of violence. Other themes recognizable from previous works include the difficulty of communication, or the impossibility thereof; the loss of innocence, and correspondingly, the discovery of different types of evil; and the occasional, apparently spontaneous incidence of cruelty or malevolence in the young.

The protagonist of the title story is the thirteen-year-old grandson of the village's one rich family. Juan's mother is involved in the endless legal complications of Spanish "divorce" (recognized separation). Because of the novelist's identification with this setting, the roughly corresponding age of her son, and her own relatively recent legal separation, it might be inferred that the story has some autobiographical basis. Such content, however, is limited to the initial situation presented, and is apparently not reflected in the plot development. At most, the story may relate what "might have been"—a flash of intuition on the writer's part, perhaps, or the sudden recognition of dangers inherent in one of the boy's activities or relationships.

Juan, like most adolescents Matute protrays, is alienated from the world of adults, disgusted by recent discoveries about his grandparents' relationship, and his grandfather's earlier amorous activities. He attempts to escape his own social milieu with its hypocritical corruption through friendship with a poor boy from a family attached to the prison camp, and so meets "el Galgo" ("Greyhound"), an older half-brother. Obviously an advanced juvenile delinquent and petty criminal, Galgo introduced the two younger boys to smoking, drinking, and apparently to marijuana or some similar drug (never identified, but implicitly present in the resultant almost hallucinatory awareness of the stars during the smoking sessions), and takes them to a house of prostitution. Juan is repelled by him and the world he represents, but somehow irresistably drawn further into the relationship which offers the only visible alternative to his morally ambivalent bourgeois existence. While it is unclear to what extent the act is drug-induced and to what extent it may be a deliberate, symbolic retribution or redistribution of wealth, the boy robs his grandparents in order to run away with Galgo, who suddenly turns on him with a knife, but then is unable to free himself from the desperate embrace or death-grip of the younger boy. Both fall into the dark waters of a nearby canal.

Such, at least, is one level of the action. The fragmentary technique and hallucinatory nature of the narrative at times suggest that nothing has really happened, that all is a nightmare or drug-induced fantasy, one of multiple possible outcomes. Whether illusion or reality, however, the message remains a clear warning of explosiveness inherent in the Spanish social structure.

Most of the stories of the collection are to some extent puzzles which the reader must assemble. In "Muy contento" ("Very Happy") the crime must be deduced from the fact that the narrator ultimately reveals his imprisonment. Apparently momentarily crazed by one clear glimpse of the past, present and future tedium of his existence, the usually docile heir to a provincial cheese factory rejected the marriage and life planned by his family and cut off his own possible retreat by burning the business. "Cuaderno para cuentas" ("The Account Book") is a stream-of-consciousness style narrative composed in an unused credit ledger by Celestina, the illegitimate duaghter of a servant and the elderly master. Having gained the favor of the lonely old man and believing she will be his heir, Celestina mixes ground glass with his food.

When her mother is blamed, the girl says nothing to save her, but too late, en route to an orphanage, discovers that she loves her.

"No tocar" ("Don't Touch"), a mixture of realism and fantasy, has a time span of some twenty years from childhood to adulthood in the life of Claudia, another cold, independent, and solitary girl. After suggestions that her personality is that of a pagan goddess who devours men, the mysterious, hermetic protagonist vanishes, to be found years later, a wooden idol worshipped by cannibals in the depths of unexplored jungle.

While infrequent in her adult fiction, there are precendents in Matute's children's books for the metamorphosis of people into objects and vice versa, a process also observable in "El rey de los Zennos" ("King of the Zennos"). This tale combines the fantastic and supernatural with a realistic setting and down-to-earth personalities with the unusual or incredible. The malign or destructive potential of creatures of fantasy becomes visible to a degree not found in Matute's writings heretofore. Ferbe, King of the Zennos, at first a goatherd and shoemaker's apprentice, exemplifies a cyclic or repetitive life principle; the time span is vague, but unquestionably covers several centuries. Ferbe is a fantastic or hallucinatory visionary, whose Messianic preaching of his kingdom-to-come causes him to be burned at the stake in an atmosphere strongly reminiscent of the Inquisition. In a subsequent later episode, he emerges from the sea, whence the wind had carried his ashes, and eventually seduces the daughter of his employer. The night before their marriage, he lured her to her death on a burning seaside pyre, and was fatally beaten by the wrathful villagers. His remains, a "bloody sponge," were washed into the sea. At an indefinite time later, he reappeared as the "King of Song" in a cheap night club, again talking of his mission or second coming. This time, Ferbe is accused of murder after having driven an enamored older woman to suicide, and the prison where he is executed is consumed by fire. Shortly after, an enormous bed of exotic sponges is discovered in the cove, and the young diver who pulls them from the water notices a strange light and senses that "something has disappeared from the earth" (p. 137). The perversion of what originally had messianic overtones suggests a connection with the Matute theme of the perversion of Christian virtue through hypocrisy. Beyond suggesting that great wrongs are done in the name of an initially harmless or good principle, however, it is risky to attribute exact interpretations. Although sufficiently different from most Matute stories to cause perplexity, it is entirely possible that "King of the Zennos" was written simply for entertainment.

"Noticias del joven K." ("News of Young K.") may initially suggest an echo of Kafka, but there is little support for this, except for the importance of guilt. "K" probably signifies Cain, as suggested both by events and the prefatory quotation from Genesis. An illegitimate peasant boy rejects all attempts at friendship by the landowner's son, who is revealed to be his half-brother, first brutally beating the younger boy, and later presumably killing him. "K" is seen hiding in the wilderness, irrational and obsessed; references to smoke, the tolling of bells, and other clues suggest that he has murdered the other, perhaps by burning. Ultimately, he is unable to exist alone, as realization of the irreparable loss of the hated but obscurely loved half-brother makes it impossible for him to go on.

"Una estrella en la piel" ("A Star on Her Skin") is a brief, enigmatic, first-person memoir by an adolescent girl who, like a horse that fascinates her, has a mark on her forehead. She intuits this mark, and a similar one on the back of a friend, as something that sets the three of them apart from others of their kind. The friend dies in an accident, and the horse is injured and has to be killed; the girl is surprised by a forest ranger while visiting the animal cemetery, and makes no outcry when dragged to a hut and raped, apparently identifying this with the fate of her two star-marked companions. A sketch in the memoir collection, *The River*, identifies the horse cemetery with the novelist's childhood realization of the meaning of death, and suggests a possible symbolic significance of the assault.

The collection calls attention anew to the maturation and increasing complexity of Matute. Fantasy and social preoccupations, the two extremes of her writing, continue to be very much in evidence, but new variations have been added to familiar themes, and her heightened technical mastery is constantly evident. *A Few Kids* may be one of her most decisive works.

CHAPTER 7

The Short Novels and Miscellaneous Works

I Fiesta al noroeste (Celebration in the Northwest)

THE FIRST of Matute's short novels, *Fiesta al noroeste*, remains one of her most interesting and typical works. Written early in her career, it obtained the "Café Gijón" prize in 1952. This prize, given by a writers' *tertulia* (regular, informal literary gathering), is unimportant financially, but carries a definite prestige value implying, as it does, the admiration of numerous artistic peers. Like *Little Theater* this work was not to appear in print for several years. It was first published by the Barcelona firm of Pareja y Borrás in 1959, and thereafter by Destino (1963 and following editions).

Celebration in the Northwest was unfavorably treated by some Spanish critics for what they adjudged a defect in construction, inasmuch as the novel begins with a rather lengthy section protagonized by Dingo, but abandons this character once he has served to introduce Juan Medinao, his one-time childhood friend, who dominates the remainder of the work and is the true protagonist. (The construction of *The Abel Family* is comparable, beginning with a narrator who subsequently vanishes, having served the purpose of "finding" Valba's diary, which constitutes the bulk of the novel.) It might be assumed that this technique characterized Matute's work of a certain early period and reflects some degree of ineptness in novelistic architecture, subsequently overcome by the mature writer. However, upon closer consideration, it seems that such is not the case; rather, it is remarkably similar to the construction utilized in her most recent novels, the two initial volumes of the trilogy *Los mercaderes (The Merchants)* in whose first part there is one protagonist, totally absent in the second part, which in turn is begun by one character but then dominated by another. Whether or not this is a defect, as argued by critics who apparently conceive the novel only in terms of a traditional, clearly structured plot, it is obviously a form for which Matute has sufficient liking to adhere to it despite unfavorable, negative criticism.

Dingo, the puppeteer, represents two constants in the novelist's work, the theme of alienation and that of the marionettes or traveling little theater. As in various of the short stories, the puppet show offers a possibility of escape, figurative or literal (as in Dingo's case), from the narrowness and tedium of life in the lonely mountain village. In *Celebration in the Northwest,* however, Matute shows the other side of the coin as well: the little theater is dingy and drab, the masks streaked with rain and dirt, the seven colors faded, and the puppeteer's cart on the verge of disintegration. Dingo has long since lost whatever illusions he had when, as a young adolescent, he absconded with the mutual savings which he and Juan Medinao were accumulating in order to leave the village together. He personifies an extreme in alienation, not only from society but also from himself, as after thirty years he no longer knows which of his many masks represents the real Dingo.

Passing by the despised village of his youth for the first time since his flight three decades ago, Dingo accidentally runs over and kills a shepherd's child, invisible until the last moment in a blinding rain. Jailed by the village authorities, he has no choice but to turn for help to Juan Medinao, whose childhood friendship he betrayed in the now distant past of both. At the moment of their encounter, Dingo all but disappears as a character, having served to provoke in Juan a series of soul-searching recollections which, together with his Holy Week confession in the present, form the bulk of the work.

Despite its compactness (130 pages), *Celebration in the Northwest* is rather complex, involving in a sense two simultaneous narratives separated by thirty years, and evoking the past of three generations of Medinaos. There is in addition a complicated symbolism: Cain and Abel, seen in the relationship of Juan Medinao and his illegitimate half-brother, Pablo; a possible Oedipal relationship (Juan and Salome, mistress of his father and mother of Pablo); the ironic, implicit symbolism of the Holy Week, Juan's confession of pride, avarice, and envy, and the final "celebration" of the child's funeral in the Northwest Cemetery.

Celebration in the Northwest is an excellent illustration of many of Matute's stylistic traits, and contains most of her constant or obsessive themes. Because of its brevity, many aspects of her art can be seen in particularly bold relief. Like the majority of her works, this is primarily a novel of childhood and adolescence, here reconstructed retrospectively by an adult protagonist. The sentiment of loss fills and overruns its pages–loss of childhood, of innocence, integrity, dreams or illusions, possessions, family, friends, even life itself. The present action of the novel (exclusive of retrospective recall or flashbacks) takes place in an almost unbroken downpour of rain, ending when the sun ironically breaks through at the burial of the child. Such heavy or prolonged rain is not characteristic of the Spanish climate, so that it must be concluded that Matute's exaggerated use of it–in all of her long novels to date except *First Memoirs*–is for purposes other than verisimilitude. Literary convention, of course, associates rain with melancholy, pessimism, or impending doom, and this tradition is in harmony with Matute's general intent, although there seems to be an additional correlation between the lowering of horizons and the closed emotional worlds of her characters.[1]

The predominant colors in *Celebration in the Northwest* are red and black, normally associated with passion and violence in the case of the former, and death or melancholy in the latter instance. The use of color is not realistic, for the most part; again the novelist seems to be seeking to create a mood, or perhaps to evoke a stylized impression of reality.[2] This can be seen particularly in her use of color to describe abstract concepts, for example, force, or the application of colors different from the usual: black fire, black lightning, red windows, a pomegranate-colored house. Among the most frequent adjectives are those expressing concepts such as solitude, loneliness, and alienation. Others express harsh, violent qualities, gloom and mystery, hostility, misery, despera-tion, malevolence, and fear. There is an almost overpowering accumula-tion of literal and figurative references to death, burial, tragedy, blood, hate, tears, cruelty, humiliation, futility, impotence, and most in-sistently, solitude.

Reinforcing this choice of language are rhetorical figures ranging from the lyrically indirect to the grotesque. Matute's typical predilec-tion for the unusual, striking, or inherently self-contradictory is seen in a frequent use of synesthesia, personification of the inanimate or non-human, and oxymoron or paradox: "burnt sounds;" "long, voiceless laments"; "frozen sparks"; "The drum of the mute, sounding like a prayer in a cave"; "his old, ill-painted life"; "the hypocritical, thieving friend, lying traveler of Nowhere"; "houses half-erased by the dirty fingers of hunger." Some of her more poetic images defy classification; "the boy, surprised by poppies" [spattered with his own blood] ; [Dingo] dragging his *fiesta* [puppeteer's cart] ; "death served up on the bed"; "winter entered through his fingernails and eyes" [on seeing his mother's corpse] ; "his shadow barely a black blink"; [The dead woman's eyes] "with many red and blue strips, like bulls with the breeder's colors in the wind"; [his strength] "like a sickness of honey"; "the pardon, made of lead, of the weak."

Many of the stark adjectives and figures of speech recall Matute's use of color, the combination suggesting an overly-stylized, primitive painting, lacking in pastels and softness, somewhat like the paintings of Solana. The world of these word paintings is entirely in harmony with the emotional world in which her characters live; hostile, uncompromising, and cold, it creates and then reflects their solitude, alienation, and despair. The relatively high degree of stylistic integration—harmonious combination of color, adjectives, rhetorical figures, and characterization—would seem to suggest either a self-conscious literary methodology, or a consistent attitude toward life.[3] The language by itself is enough to call to mind an existentialist vision of the radical solitude of the individual; this is reinforced by the nature of the characters themselves and their interaction with their environment and those around them. Whether philosophically conceived, or merely intuited, this combination of elements adds up to a picture sufficiently coherent and characteristic that various critics have referred to it as "the world" of Matute.[4]

The various characters of *Celebration in the Northwest*, with the exception of Pablo Zácaro, represent extremes of loneliness and alienation; Pablo, unusually independent and self-sufficient, is alone but not lonely. Dingo's alienation is increased by the accident, which places him in the situation of an offender against society, guilty before the law although through no real fault of his own. This intensifies the loneliness of a lifetime, unrelieved by the overly-pious aid subsequently promised by Juan Medinao, whose act of charity is more a vengeance and humiliation than an example of Christian forgiveness. In his own way, the latter is equally lonely and alienated. His birth—the only son of the one rich family in La Artámila—and his physical deformity are factors which have from the beginning estranged him from the villagers. His family life was a private hell, with his mother reputed to be crazy and his father a brutal drunk whose role as the village Don Juan drove his mother to suicide when Juan Niño was five. The boy is obsessively conscious that he is "different," to the extent that he eventually comes to feel that he has no connection with the human race. The one ephemeral friendship of his childhood was with Dingo, a relationship motivated largely by Dingo's desire to exploit the boy economically in order to make possible his own escape from La Artámila. Grown to manhood, Juan secretly despised everyone, disguising this behind a mask of Christian asceticism, and comforting himself in his solitude with the conviction of his moral superiority.

The one exception to his indifference, his illegitimate half-brother Pablo Zácaro, was the object of an obscure love-hate mixed with the suggestion of repressed homosexual desires. Pablo, the disinherited but envied and talented younger son, plays Abel to Juan's Cain, and Juan's attempts to dominate Pablo are the real substance of the novel. He does not attack Pablo physically, but makes varied efforts to attract him, to bribe, to coerce and to otherwise influence Pablo, always with the purpose of bringing him to his house, and symbolically to submission. He finally buys Pablo's fiancée, Delia, with gifts and promises made to her parents, destitute tenant-farmers, hoping that her presence will attract Pablo, and even conveying through Salome, Pablo's mother, an implicit willingness to "share" the girl. This failing, Juan rapes Salome, in a moment when he is overwhelmed by her resemblance to Pablo.

Social undertones of the Cain-Abel motif are seen when Pablo organizes the peasants in a strike against Juan; most are soon reduced to submission, but Pablo goes to the city, leaving Juan a hollow victory which is really defeat as it has put Pablo definitively beyond his reach. Another implication of this motif appears in the exclusivity of religious sentiment: as a child, Juan was troubled at the thought he might have to share God with the intruder, Pablo—perhaps an oblique but comprehensible reference to the attitude of the Spanish church hierarchy during and immediately after the Civil War.

The general atmosphere of loneliness and alienation is upheld in the characterization of secondary figures such as Dingo's mute and mentally retarded assistant, who represents an extreme of inability to comprehend or communicate with a hostile world. Juan's mother, whether insane or not as reputed, was as estranged from her surroundings as if she were insane since she was treated as a psychotic; she felt that she was "buried alive in the village, and lonely as the dead." The father, Juan Padre, despite his brutality and infidelities, is an almost pitiful case of emotional ineptness and inability to communicate.

The plot line is rather tenuous; Matute is more concerned with psychological aspects than with action as such. The situation of Dingo is left somewhat unresolved, although it is implied that Juan Medinao will use his money and influence with the easily corruptible local authorities in order to extricate Dingo as an oblique means of punishing him for his long-ago betrayal. This framework action need not be definitively resolved, however; it exists mainly for the purpose of introducing Juan and partially explaining his character. The boy's death serves to bring a priest to the village, too poor to maintain a church, and thus makes possible Juan's confession. The technique of interweaving confession and memories reveals Juan's insincerity, showing that his confession is misleading in its incompleteness.

Juan represents two aspects of the established order of Spanish society: the decayed, landowning aristocracy, and the rural *cacique* (political boss). If he is to some extent a symbolic figure, it is worth noting that despite his ugliness, deformities, and moral deterioration the novelist is not unsympathetic in her treatment of him. In view of undertones in later works, it should be considered significant that he in effect hides behind religiosity most of his life, and that immediately after the climax of the novel (retrospective recall of his rape of Salome), Juan ends his confession accusing himself of gluttony and laziness, but with no mention of his crime. He receives absolution, and whatever symbolic comment the novelist may wish to make on the relationship between the system he represents and the church must be deduced from a single, final sentence observing that the following day he could receive communion and "hear the bells." It should be borne in mind that *Celebration in the Northwest* was written during a period of extreme censorship, and that in any case, Matute is too much of an artist to indulge in propaganda or invective. Nevertheless, a clearly critical attitude is conveyed to the attentive reader.

There is a long preface to the French edition of the novel *Fête au Nord-Ouest* (Paris: Gallimard, 1961) by translator Elena de la Souchère, in which she studies the themes and modes of expression of Matute, reaching the conclusion that the major themes are childhood and death. The narrow world of La Artámila is seen by the translator as the symbol of a limited. closed-in Spain, where one can only resign oneself to living. The prefatory study also notes a "superabundance of images, an apparent verbal delirium [wherein] not a single word is useless or irrelevant to the action, because lines, colors, sounds, gestures, odors, all the sensory notations replacing the classical psychological analysis, are charged with creating the environment and translating the state of mind of the characters."

Another article, also apropos of the French translation, uses *Celebration in the Northwest* as a starting point for a brief study of Matute's works, identifying as essential themes the attachment to the land versus the desire to flee it, and the opposition of brothers.[5] This observer sees the Matute characters as not yet adults, paralyzed by memories, obsessed and fixated by experiences from which they cannot free themselves, immobilized in time, with the shadow of death ever menacingly present.

For the most part, *Celebration in the Northwest* received little significant critical notice, either serving as a stepping stone for discussion of other works, or being the object of reviews which consisted of no more than summaries of the plot. The long-inedited work was published and translated largely as a result of the success of *The Dead Children*, and while it thus benefitted from the interest in Matute's writing as a whole, it was neglected as an entity in itself.

II Tres y un sueño[6] (Three [Fantasies] and a Dream)

There are three independent narratives in this volume, all rather fantastic in nature. The "dream" is presumably childhood, for which the three tales illustrate possible endings: a child who grows up (Ivo), a child who dies (Perico), and a child who refuses to grow up psychologically, even though she matures physically (the "Black Sheep"). The dream-like quality of childhood is conveyed by the similarly unreal atmosphere of the stories. In the first, "La razón" ("Reason"), the world is that of fairy tales and fantasy. In "La isla" ("The Island"), there are elements of magic and the supernatural, and in the third, "La oveja negra" ("The Black Sheep"), strange, surrealistic, nightmarish situations abound. All three have a certain timelessness, causing the impression that "normal" time has been abolished, yet time does not stand still, as clearly shown by the growing up of Ivo, the death of Perico, and the fact that the girl "Black Sheep" one day finds herself a mother.

Reason is an attribute apparently imcompatible with childhood and the powers of fantasy; possessing it is symbolically associated with growing up, with childhood's end. The orphaned dreamer, Ivo, solitary and imaginative, was able to see the only three gnomes left in the world, invisible to more "reasonable" individuals. Because the existence of gnomes depends on the credulity of a human believer "with moondrops in his eyes," the dwarf Tano took Ivo on a tour of the magic world of eternal spring, so that he might never wish to stop dreaming. However, the visit so impressed the boy that he was on the verge of dying of sadness and his resultant inability to exist in the world of reality. Realizing that if Ivo dies the dwarfs would be doomed in any case, Tano took away his imagination by removing the moondrops from his eyes. The gnomes were turned to ashes and Ivo, cured, returned to ask the farmer for work, stating that he now is using reason. This is symbolically conveyed by his purchase of his first pair of long pants. A more sophisticated and artistic version of material treated frequently in the juvenilia, "Reason" repeats the symbol used in *The Stupid Children* whereby long pants signify having ceased to live in the magic world of childhood.

The action of "The Island" takes place in a realm of initially greater reality, without dwarfs and gnomes or conversations with the moon, a world in which a little boy playing hooky is robbed of his coat and shoes, and swindled by a sideshow operator at a fair. Nevertheless, this is a world where the marvelous exists, at least for little Perico who, by hitting the bull's-eye three times at the fair, won an island for himself and saw it rise magically from the sea. The island, however, is a symbol of death (the child froze without his clothes), as indicated by the weeping in Perico's house, and the fact that his nurse had to look for other work. Many years later, when Aya, the old nurse, has been sent to a home for the aged, Perico's visit to her with his island signifies her death also, though both events are told with such lyrical indirectness as probably to escape the comprehension of many readers. Several elements present herein may be seen also in the children's tale, "The Green Grasshopper," and here, as in Matute's juvenile fiction, there are occasional distant echoes of Hans Christian Andersen (a case in point is the power of innocence: Perico is able to hit the bull's-eye because he has never engaged in deception).

"The Black Sheep" has been considered strange and puzzling by many readers. While some critics have believed it to be a kind of surrealistic experiment and others have dismissed it essentially without comment, at least one perspicacious observer noted that it must have an autobiographical basis.[7] Some seventy pages in length, this novelette has as its protagonist a fantastic, introspective girl, "bad" in the eyes of her family because she is different and solitary, with a great love of the forest. Her one companion—and only briefly—is a puppet which she fashioned herself, Tomboctu. One night Tomboctu was torn up by the dog, Lucio, who died after the girl caressed him. Although she knows what has become of Tomboctu, she nevertheless endlessly seeks and calls him, strangely never attempting to make another. The girl suffers a prolonged and serious illness, finally arising after the visit of two black brothers who invite her to accompany them in search of Tomboctu. Because of the relationship between the boys, she eventually identifies them as Cain and Abel. Exposed, they flee, abandoning her in the forest.

Certain parallels can be noted between the story line to this point and the girlhood history of Matute: the introspective and solitary character of "Black Sheep," her love of the forest, the black doll, the prolonged childhood illness, and the Civil War (represented by Cain and Abel). The search for Tomboctu, initiated as it is after Cain and Abel's visit—i.e., after the war—may symbolize the effort to recapture her lost childhood, or perhaps to recover certain ideals and illusions forever destroyed by the conflict. At this juncture there is a break in the relatively linear nature of the chronology; simultaneously, the girl's adventures become more confusing for her and consequently for the reader. There begins a series of encounters and wanderings with various figures, probably representative of important relationships in the novelist's life. The overall effect of this prolonged journey is something between a pilgrimage and a picaresque novel.

Beyond the river, "Black Sheep" saw the cart of a puppeteer with whom she traveled, sharing his meals. Disappointed to find that his marionette theater was an illusion, she accused him of deceit and the puppets were mysteriously broken. Finally arriving at the sea, they met a procession of gypsy penitents carrying a figure of Christ. The girl feels no repentance, alleging that she has never sinned, but she is called unworthy and asked to leave. Believing she sees Tomboctu, she runs after him but finds only a wooden cross. The marionette theater is a constant in the work of Matute, and the discovery that this, too, involved deception is significantly equated with the end of childhood. The momentary, erroneous identification of Tomboctu with the wooden cross may refer to an adolescent mysticism or religiosity of brief duration.

Wandering, "Black Sheep" comes upon a group of shacks and approaches because she is hungry. After sharing their humble fare, she is expected to help the women and told not to criticize the men. The episode is obviously symbolic of initiation into Spanish womanhood. She learns "you must always say yes, keep quiet and agree" (p. 95). This scene is shattered by soldiers who herd the men onto a train, gunning down those who attempt to escape. She is irritated by the passivity of the women who allow themselves to be enclosed near the military camp, return promptly to routine, and even establish relationships with the soldiers. This may be inspired by some particular postwar reprisals of the Franco regime, but probably symbolized an outcry against all those (and particularly her own generation) who in these years accepted repression and allowed it to become a normal way of life.

One day she is fascinated by a strange, silent soldier, believing that she sees Tomboctu around his neck. Attempting to grasp the doll (illusion of happiness), she is forced to accompany the soldier (a probable symbolic reference to her marriage), but later realized there is nothing around his neck but a dirty, discolored coin. Much later, after he is killed, she finds the bullet-shattered coin and saves it "for when I am sad or afraid" (p. 104). Perhaps the coin symbolized the writer's profession, shared by the novelist with her husband, a pursuit which became for a time a refuge for her.

One morning she realizes there is a child with her who calls her "Mother." The boy slowly grows up and one day catches a black horse and leaves her, probably symbolic of that dreaded future time when her son—who answers to the name of Tomboctu, childhood's illusion recaptured—will cease to be a child. One important episode involves her taking the child to church, a cathedral filled with venerable, weeping ancients, which is attacked by a hungry mob. She sees how old, decadent, and deteriorated are the formerly impressive furnishings (no doubt representing a critical attitude toward the immensely wealthy Spanish church with its idle treasures in the midst of widespread poverty).

After losing the boy, her adventures become progressively sadder; she is the object of ridicule and cruel jokes. Exhausted and sick, she is found in a vacant lot by her brothers who pay a boy to carry food to her. Curious, the children of the village follow him and eventually become her consolation, for although they play at "killing" her, their lily-leaf swords are harmless, and she knows this game will last so long as they do not grow up. In this conclusion, there is some distant echo of Peter Pan, as "Black Sheep" insists until the end that she is a child, which is what separates her definitively from the more normal world. While it is not necessary to seek a symbolic referent for the village children, they could easily represent those young readers for whom Matute destines her juvenile fiction.

J. Villa Pastur's review of *Tres y un sueño, (Three Fantasies and a Dream)* in *La Voz de Asturias* (Oviedo, April 11, 1961) stated that Matute's work "revolves exclusively around the problems raised by the passage from childhood to youth . . . we witness a disintegration of the magical concept of life." Perhaps due to the nature of the work, the high dosage of fantasy and obscurity, it was largely overlooked by Spanish critics or handled with extreme brevity and superficiality, and has gone almost entirely unnoticed outside Spain. There is one useful, but relatively inaccessible article by Angel Marsá in the Barcelona newspaper, *El correo catalán* for April 23rd, 1961, which observes that

Matute is "herself one more literary figure in her dark painting, identified with the smallest creatures and the greatest tragedies ... [her] men and women who are older boys and girls or boys and girls who are premature men and women, betrayed by life ... and victims of all existential anguish."

II   Libro de juegos para los niños de los otros[8]
(Book of Games for the Others' Children)

This is an unusual and interesting work consisting of a brief, ironic text accompanied by J. Buesa's full-page photographs of children of the street in black and white. The "others" are the poor, and the book is quite possibly Matute's most eloquent indictment of class prejudice and poverty, two evils which rob these children of true childhood. The style is her simplest, most unadorned and straightforward; the point of view (as in *The Stupid Children*) is usually that of the child, but the poetic element is lacking. There is an almost total absence of long or involved sentences or ideas, and metaphors are few and simple, creating a poor and childlike syntax. With less than thirty pages, unnumbered and often half-empty, the impact is disproportionate to its size. The lower-class child is a familiar figure in Matute's works, but the pathos and hopelessness of existence for these children has frequently been blurred by the presence of a plot or a more rhetorical and decorative prose. In *Book of Games* the stark simplification intensifies the reader's awareness of the barren tragedy underlying the games of children without toys, almost without clothes, often hungry and dirty, necessarily left alone by working parents to invent their own amusements.

The "games" are of two types, those invented by the children—to forget hunger or the futile anger of parents frustrated by inability to feed them—and the "games people play," such as "charity" and religion. These children play along with the "catechism game" because they are given bread and jelly. The "crucifixion game" exemplifies the Matute theme of spontaneous cruelty in children: the crucifixion of bats, stray dogs, and kittens. False or insufficient charity is exposed in "The Game of Desire" in which the poor child is given a sweater at Christmas and left with a thousand unfulfilled desires. In the "Game of Envy" a band of poor boys watch the games of the rich beyond an iron fence. The "Game of Deception" is learned early, as the children of the poor are frequently sent to tell stories to excuse the inability to pay. The most "Dangerous Game" is not played frequently: thinking about life and growing up.

IV   El río[9] (The River)

Usually described as memoirs, this book consists of some fifty sketches, unrelated by story line or chronology, but with geographical and emotional unity. The setting is once more Mansilla de la Sierra; besides the nostalgia with which Matute normally views her childhood, *The River* is tinged with melancholy because of the definitive loss of that beloved landscape beneath the waters of a recently constructed reservoir. For the novelist, the lake and awkward new village are not reality, however: reality continues to exist beneath the waters' calm surface, in the submerged village, in the river which still runs toward "somewhere from whence there is no return, like life." The river thus becomes a link with the past, and a symbol of time, a conventional symbolism, but here endowed with unusual feeling and lyricism.

The River is particularly useful as a source of autobiographical reminiscences and further description of the life of the Castilian peasant. Various inspirations for subsequent narrations can be detected, as well as clues to the symbolic meaning the novelist attaches to such figures as the fox, dog, and wolf. Other passages illuminate her attitude toward the cruelty of children, and the novelist's feeling about death, particularly the death of children. There are references to the traditional rural Castilian celebrations of birth, marriage, and funerals, to typical peasant attitudes and reactions, and such surviving ancient customs as the ritual use of communal ovens. More than a dozen complete, brief narratives, similar to those in *Tales of Artámila,* reveal that much real experience underlies Matute's tales; Mansilla was a veritable fountainhead of narrative potential, and she had the necessary awareness and sensitivity to realize it. There are prose poems containing lyric descriptions of the village, its people, or a secret spot beloved in childhood. Various sections are duplicated in *Halfway Down the Road,* usually described as "chronicles."

V   A la mitad del camino[10] (Halfway Down the Road)

It is difficult to classify this collection of articles and sketches, many largely autobiographical. Some are meditative or confessional in nature, while a few are more journalistic or approach literary criticism. The book, published in a limited edition, is of difficult access; most likely it was not considered a commercial venture. It has no unity of theme, place, or time, although some coherence derives from the fact that almost all the ingredients have some special meaning or importance for the novelist. Perhaps its nature is best conveyed by Matute's own words, that she will "empty her pockets, mentally, of things kept until now without really knowing why," of experiences, fear, or amazement, surprise, nostalgia, hope, "in case any of it might be utilized some time" (pp. 9-10). This book is unusually revealing of her character and personality and, as is *The River*, it is a treasurehouse of hints as to the associations and symbolic values attached by the novelist to such things as the toad and the wolf; the significance of cruelty in children; the importance of humble objects normally used and discarded without a thought. Another sketch expresses her idea that things show their true selves when sleeping. There are brief, personal essays on the importance of silence, of memory, and sadness: "We could not live, surely, without those moments of necessary melancholy, without nostalgia. For a man or a woman without memories must resemble nothing more than an empty trunk" (p. 33).

There are meditations on time, on heat, the death of a dog, even on mud, with its different substances and the attraction it holds for a child. Several sketches are protagonized by puppets or dolls, and another expounds the author's long-standing interest in the strolling players and marionette theater. Others are directly related to her son, or have as their subject children in general. "Sobre el niño, estos días" ("On Children, This Time of Year"), written at school's reopening in the fall, and undoubtedly the result of her own unpleasant schoolday memories, is a plea for more understanding and the recognition that children are often in the right. Various other ideas on children, such as the essential solitude of the child, the irremediable separation between child and adult worlds, and the total difference between childhood and adulthood, are here expressed much more clearly than in her narrative works. Matute also lyrically extols trees, the importance and even necessity of lies (dreams, illusions), and as in so many other works, returns obsessively to the theme of the death of a child. The thirty-four separate pieces are mostly evocative or contemplative, with little or no narrative content. While some, particularly the last few, refer specifically to the present, most are retrospective. A few themes emerge again and again: time (time as memory, and the passing of time), death, childhood (her own and childhood in general), the importance of the past, and illusion.

Only one article, "La caridad" ("Charity"), eludes the autobiographical or confessional categories. This too is highly personal, despite a more objective inspiration, revealing Matute's aspirations toward social justice, and explaining what she understands by true and false charity. True charity exists only with love, and the novelist is horrified by that ostentatious "charity." which humiliates the receiver. Charity, she explains, is more than money: it is being a patient listener, giving a chance, pardoning the faults of others, refusing to listen to gossip, and "sometimes, perhaps, not believing in evil" (p. 58), characteristics which she finds all too infrequent in the "charity" usually offered in Spain.

While largely lacking in narrative interest and relatively unpretentious artistically, *Halfway Down the Road* offers such a wealth of insights and explanations of the meaning things hold for Matute as to make its perusal quite rewarding.

Whether due to the largely non-narrative nature, or because they were published in limited editions and probably not considered major works. *The River, Halfway Down the Road,* and *Book of Games . . .* have been all but totally ignored by the critics.

VI   *The Children's Fiction*

According to the novelist, she first began inventing stories for the entertainment of her son, increasing the level of difficulty as he grew, and almost without conscious planning on her part found herself launched on another writing venture. The order of publication of the juvenile stories does not follow an ascending order of intellectual difficulty; of course, they may not be part of the group originally composed for her son. Matute's juvenile fiction generally shows characteristics common to the unpublished juvenilia and to her writing for adults, especially the tales of fantasy. Frequent use of the orphan characterizes all levels of her work; in the juvenile fiction, even an animal protagonist loses his mother. The only exception to this rule in the works for children is *El país de la pizarra*[11] *(Blackboard Land)* intended for the youngest audience. The characteristic concern for social justice is presented on levels a child can understand in *Paulina, el mundo y las estrellas*[12] *(Pauline, the World and the Stars)* and *El polizón del "Ulises"*[13] *(The Cabin Boy of the "Ulysses").* There are other themes which are essentially the same in all her writings, so that reference to the juvenile fiction will in some cases bring into clearer relief aspects of Matute's writing for adults.

El saltamontes verde[14] *(The Green Grasshopper)* recalls themes of the juvenilia, recounting the search of orphaned Yungo for his voice. He discovers that it was stolen at his birth by a talking grasshopper, his long-time companion, for the purpose of doing good in the world. The child renounces recuperation of his voice rather than kill the *saltamontes,* and flies to the "Beautiful Land" to rejoin his parents. As he is an orphan, this presumably means the death of the boy, but Matute presents it in a lyric and indirect fashion which recalls similar portrayals in *The Stupid Children*. Map and island motives in this story resemble those in "The Island," found in the collection *Three Fantasies and a Dream*. The end of childhood, often coinciding with the renunciation of a cherished illusion, is frequently represented by Matute as the death of a child.

"El aprendiz" ("The Apprentice") appears in the same volume. The atmosphere of this tale is definitely reminiscent of Hans Christian Andersen. An embittered old miser agrees to accept a strange orphan as his apprentice since the boy possesses the talent of sweeping up gold, which he gives to his master, asking only to work for the townspeople in his spare time to earn his meals. The story's object is to teach that money is not important in itself but for the things that one does with it, as the miser eventually learns. The opposition between materialism and idealism which underlies the story, and concretely the opposition between idealism and money, is an oft-repeated theme in Matute's work. The miser eventually learns his lesson, and in so doing changes from a hard-bitten adult to the simplicity and gentleness of a child, so that his ultimate death is treated lyrically, like those of children. The closeness of the very old and young is a frequent topic in children's literature, and one that Matute has used several times. The saving power of repentance, symbolized by tears, found in many of Andersen's fairy tales (including Matute's favorite, "The Snow Queen") is seen in "The Apprentice."

Pauline, the World and the Stars is a full-length novel for adolescent girls, the author's longest work for younger readers. Its tone, setting, and aspects of plot recall that timeless classic, *Heidi*. The novel is the first-person memoir of twelve-year-old Paulina, an orphan who goes to live with her grandparents in the mountains while convalescing from a serious illness. The setting is, in all probability, the same familiar Castilian mountain village of Matute's childhood, most closely approximating the portrayal in *Tales of Arámila*. There are two principal narrative threads: Paulina's discovery of economic and social inequities ("The World") and of nature, the seasons, timeless beauty ("The Stars"). The social themes are seen in Paulina's friendship with "Nin," blind son of sharecroppers, who spends winters with her grandparents because his health cannot withstand the cold in his family's dilapidated cabin. There are many notes common to Matute's usual presentation of village life: the struggle for existence among peasants tilling an unyielding land which, after generations, still is not theirs; the vicious cycle of poverty and ignorance endlessly repeating itself as poor children must leave school to work; the women who must tie newborn babies to their backs while working the fields, or leave them alone. "That's the way the land is; it takes everything" (p. 119). The eventual solution—Paulina's decision to renounce what she will inherit from her grandparents in favor of the peasants—is probably overoptimistic and facile, but it suggests to young readers that something can be done about social injustice and inequity, at least on the individual level. Matute's ideal of justice is here carried to its most explicit level in all her writing.

Blackboard Land is intended for a much younger audience. It too recalls parts of the juvenilia, especially those tales reflecting the boredom of the child faced with homework and the resulting escapes through fantasy. Without being in any sense a copy, this story probably owes some of its inspiration to *Through the Looking Glass*: a similar, absurdly logical fantasy land lies right within the realm of the child's daily existence, in this case beyond the blackboard. The novelist's capacity for fantasy and her understanding of children are evident in the description of the "City of Multiplication Tables" with its endless noise of calculators and numeral-citizens, each performing specific functions suggested by their shapes. Matute both expresses a tacit sympathy with those problems that loom so large for children (all but forgotten by adults), and suggests that these must be met and solved by children themselves. Avoiding all semblance of preachment, she removes many of their negative associations, and so exemplifies her own theory of a more positive and less catechistically solemn children's literature than that previously available in Spain.

Caballito loco[15] *(Little Crazy Horse)* is no exception to that sentimentality that suffuses many animal stories. In many ways the animal protagonist resembles human adolescents portrayed elsewhere by the novelist: he is different, solitary, a "loner," living in a dream world which enables him to retain his pureness of heart despite an evil environment. He preserves a child's spirit, and like many Matute children, achieves his dream at the cost of his life. The steadfast and unending devotion of Little Crazy Horse to a cruel and ungrateful bandit eventually leads to his death, but his supreme sacrifice is rewarded by the master's ultimate, if tardy, recognition of the animal's love.

Carnavalito (Little Carnival) appears in the same slender volume. Here one may detect a faint echo of another classic, "The Pied Piper of Hamelin." There is a striking parallel between the two processions, each led by a Harlequin-clad musician, whose playing weaves a spell. The differences, however, are numerous, and whether or not Matute was inspired by the legend, *Little Carnival* is an original creation. Then, too, she has used similar Harlequin figures frequently elsewhere, and this may simply be another manifestation. In this tale, the novelist strikes a blow against chauvinistic regionalism, characteristic of Spanish villagers, and the superstitious suspicion of red hair. The townspeople insisted that Bongo, orphan apprentice of a redhaired blacksmith, was being beaten and starved. The smith explained: 'Neither you nor I was born here. They don't know where we come from, and they are people who must touch things with their hands to believe in them" (p.52).

Despite elements of timeless legend, *Little Carnival* is very definitely set in the twentieth century, with war scenes reminiscent of the Spanish civil conflict. The bulk of the narrative concerns the search of a procession of children, mostly war orphans, for the Promised Land of Peace. In the deceptively simple context of a children's fantasy, Matute expresses one of the profound preoccupations and aspirations of her generation of writers, transcending the horrors of the Civil War and the still-unhealed breach between the former belligerents. Symbolically, hope is made to rest upon the children, citizens of the future, who will one day cultivate the Land of Peace.

The Cabin Boy of "Ulysses," Matute's most recent children's book, quotes *Peter Pan* on its frontispiece: "All the children of the world, save one, grow up," And this is the story of some decisive moments and days in which a childhood ended, the story of a little boy who grew up. The theme is one of the novelist's favorites, whether presented wistfully and nostalgically (as in most of the writing for adults), or more positively, as a challenge, in her children's literature. Her insistence on that decisive experience which, at whatever age, effectively marks the end of childhood, evinces her continuing preoccupation with that event in her own childhood, still insufficiently comprehended, when the Civil War ended what had been a magic world. Often symbolized by Matute as the death of a child, that moment seems at last to acquire a positive potential in *The Cabin Boy. . .*

This setting also resembles the same familiar "Artámila"—there are similarities in the house, outbuildings, village, river and forest, the surrounding mountains, and the penal camp visible from the attic observation post of Juju, the boy-hero. The main action of the book concerns the escape of a prisoner, coinciding with a wolf hunt. This and the rather primitive rural celebration after the death of a wolf recall similar moments in *The Dead Children*. The prisoner is subsequently hunted in much the same fashion. Juju shelters the fugitive and helps him to escape, hoping to see the world with him. Ultimately, the man renounces his freedom in order to take home the sick boy whom he had intended to abandon. Convalescent, the child finds he is now treated "like a man." It is discovered that none of his former clothes fit; even the boots are too small. This symbolic growth, similar to that of "The Boy Whose Friend Died" in *The Stupid Children*, is less common than the metaphoric representation of childhood's end as the death of a child, but significant in its reflection of a more positive attitude toward such moments. The fact that this is a recent expression may indicate that the novelist is beginning to overcome lingering negative feelings associated with her own traumatic "growing up overnight." It is worth noting that *The Cabin Boy* . . . (together with the other juvenile fiction) lacks that pessimism so often noted in Matute's writing for adults. While true childhood is one thing about which she does not seem to be pessimistic on any level, the ending of *The Cabin Boy* . . . indicates a definite optimism about, and acceptance of, ending childhood. Since the time of composition closely coincides with that of the second volume of the trilogy, *The Merchants*, wherein other positive notes emerge in the adult fiction, it can legitimately be suggested as a landmark in the novelist's personal emotional evolution.

CHAPTER 8

Maturity: Los hijos muertos (The Dead Children)

I *Matute's Literary Tenets*

FROM THE early fifties until well into the sixties, most young writers in Spain were influenced by *objetivismo* "Objectivism," an outgrowth of the French experimental "new novel" or *nouveau roman.* This movement, generally far left politically and having vague philosophical affinities with Existentialism, held that the psychological novel was a vein which had been mined out, and that anyway it was impossible to see inside another human being (the Existentialist concept of radical solitude and the impossibility of communication). Therefore, Objectivist writers concentrated on the external—words, actions, and the description of *objects*, attempting to achieve scientific exactness. Influenced by the developing movie industry, particularly the Italian Neo-Realist cinema, they tried to present in the novel the same data that might be reproduced by a movie camera with sound track, striving to eliminate all subjectivity—the author's personality, judgments, analyses, and beliefs. Interpretation and evaluation should be left to the reader. The adherent of Objectivism would never assert that "María felt sad," but instead present her gazing into the distance, heaving a sigh, with perhaps a tear rolling down her cheek. With these clues, the reader must then reach his own conclusions.

While initial interest in the movement may have sprung from aesthetic impulses, young Spanish writers soon realized its possibilities against the censorship. Their apparently impassive, cryptic descriptions of "facts" were difficult to censor on the usual moral, religious, or political grounds. Objectivist techniques were adopted almost at once by the so-called Social Realists as a means of presenting their social (a euphemism for political) criticisms. Such "objective" presentation of social injustice and inequity came very close to the thesis novel, albeit necessarily without direct preachment or editorializing.

The Social Realists concentrated on depicting the miserable living and working conditions of the lower classes, and at the opposite extreme, presented the lives of the bourgeoisie as immoral, egotistical, and parasitical. Characters were usually sterotyped: the basically good, long-suffering, and exploited poor (proletariat), and the corrupt, selfish, and empty rich (capitalists). The resulting literature is gray, repetitive in themes, characters, and treatment, and (intrusion of the writer's subjectivity being taboo), limited in personality and originality. Therefore unappealing to the general public, the movement by 1962 or 1963 had begun to decline. As early as 1962, the late Martín Santos[1] realized the limitations of this literary fashion, and called attention to the need to find new channels for the future development of the Spanish novel. Nevertheless, this style of writing continued to find exponents for several years longer.

Ana María Matute is a strongly individualistic, personal, and subjective writer, and many Objectivist tenets conflicted with her personal concept of the novel. She is independent enough to be little influenced by literary fashions, despite her sharing many of the ideals of the Social Realists. "To me, literary fads seem stupid. I always say something which is silly but, I think, quite true: that there are only two kinds of novels, good and bad, and nothing else matters. All techniques are good when the writer is good, and technique has nothing to do with it when the writer is bad. So it is that Objectivism is good in the novels of Robbe-Grillet, but used by a bad writer, it is catastrophic," she observed, and then explained her own position: "In any case, for me it is not enough. For my way of viewing the novel, Objectivism is exaggerated. Besides, I absolutely do not believe in it. My eyes will always be *my* eyes, and very likely see differently."[2] As Matute realized, each writer is a human being, not a machine, and complete objectivity in the perception and description of objects and events is obviously impossible. And of course the explicit social ends invalidate from the outset any claim to real objectivity.

However, Matute did not reject Objectivism entirely. She agreed with the movement's criticism that past authors intruded too much into their works, addressing the reader directly, presenting opinions, digressing, and praising or condemning characters and events. "That business of a writer's being totally inserted in his books, as happened with the author's intervention in some novels of the past, is no good either. I am in favor of Objectivism, but a more human version. And naturally a writer is always present in his works, though he may try to avoid it."[3] Matute's books from the mid-fifties on showing a continuing and increasing social preoccupation, and her own individualized style and techniques are increasingly combined with a modified, personal form of Objectivism. The novelist has on various occasions endorsed the social aims of the postwar Spanish novel: " . . . in the epoch in which we live . . . literature which is purely entertainment has no reason for existing. I believe the writer has in his charge a social function, and that the novel has always been social, it cannot help but be."[4] Her own novels were "almost all, if not all, a protest," with the exception of some of the works of fantasy. Spanish censorship tends to become more lenient in proportion to a writer's increasing fame (as more opportunities become available for publishing outside Spain), and thus in Matute's later works the social criticism is somewhat more open. Although present in some degree in earlier works, these social aims, together with the influences of Objectivism and the Social Realists, can be most plainly seen in *The Dead Children* and subsequent novels.

II   Los hijos muertos[5] (The Dead Children)

Matute worked from 1951 to 1958 on *The Dead Children*, her monumental novel of the Civil War. It is not the typical war novel, since the conflict serves largely as background while the novelist focusses on its effects upon the lives of the children and adolescents of two generations, as well as tentatively exploring the causes, a still unresolved and explosive series of underlying social factors. Again using the landscape of Old Castile, the more than five hundred pages of *The Dead Children* incorporate much of the novelist's personal experience. The peasants and their often picturesque customs are the same she came to know as a child. The prison camp which figures so prominently is the one mentioned in "Los chicos," located not far from her grandmother's house. Young Ana María had frequently talked with the head of the penal colony (the model for Diego Herrera), the prison officers, and civil guards, as well as the wives of the prisoners who lived, as the novel relates, in fragile shacks by the river. But the real inspiration for the novel came as she observed the return of the exiles in the years after the Civil War and realized that problems were unchanged, and that the returning exiles and her generation had much in common.

The Dead Children was published in 1958 and won the "Premio de la Crítica," the "Critics' Prize" which, being unendowed, enjoys a reputation for impartiality. It is perhaps the most prestigious literary award in Spain, and the critics' selection of *The Dead Children* as the best novel of 1958 was definitely Matute's most significant recognition to that date. Previously, she had received few critical notices, and only one translation, the 1951 *Infidele alla terra (Unfaithful to the Land),* Italian version of *The Abel Family.* Matute began to be the object of more reviews, interviews, and critical studies, and these multiplied still further when *The Dead Children* was "officially" recognized, becoming the recipient of the Miguel de Cervantes National Literary Prize for 1959. As Matute also won the Premio Nadal in 1959 (for *Primera memoria,* submitted under a pseudonym), the resulting publicity, aided by polemics over the Nadal award, made her one of the country's best-known writers. Foreign attention was drawn to her work, and translations were begun of several books published previously, resulting in considerable international dissemination from 1960 on.[6] Having received both the Critics' Prize and National Literary Prize, *The Dead Children* became one of Spain's most honored novels since the Civil War. Undoubtedly this factor favored Matute when, also in 1959, she was selected by the March Foundation (which awards grants to prominent authors to assist with work in progress) as the recipient of fifty thousand pesetas to further the writing of her projected trilogy, *Los mercaderes (The Merchants).*

Much more ambitious and complex than earlier works (or than any of her novelistic undertakings, unless the trilogy be considered as a whole), *The Dead Children* is, in the opinion of many critics, Matute's masterpiece to date. Certainly it is one of her most significant achievements. She attempts to present a broad social fresco, representing various class levels, as well as both victors and vanquished in the Civil War. *The Dead Children* recalls cyclic or stream-of-consciousness "family" novels of earlier in the century, offering a panorama of several generations of the Corvo family, although concentrating on its last remnants. These are three generations in the years immediately before, during, and after the civil conflict. But the Corvos, despite their prominent role, are not the real protagonists: most of them are archetypes, and taken in the total setting, of which the sharecroppers and villagers are part, they are symbolic of all of rural Spain. The narrative function of the Corvos recalls *The Abel Family* and *Celebration in the Northwest,* among other works, as their story serves as a sort of overture—and possible camouflage—for that of Miguel Fernández, the true protagonist. Time, and the differing generations, are important for comprehension of the novel's total import, as are such key symbols as the crow and the wolf.

Few critics have remarked how much *The Dead Children* owes to *In This Land*—or more specifically, to the censored version, *The Fireflies,* the immediately preceding full-length novel. While there is no overlap of plot, and the technique of the later work is much more sophisticated and complex, the basic inspiration, creative impulse, and underlying sentiment seem nearly identical. Likewise, both works in their settings combine Barcelona and the scene of the novelist's childhood summers, a peculiarity not found to date in any other novel. The scope of *The Dead Children* is somewhat larger, but both novels study the same period and attempt a nonpartisan, personal stance, while showing more sympathy for the losers than admiration for the winners. In each, the military conflict is relegated to a plane of importance secondary to the war's effects upon individuals, what war means, the pain, hurt, and absurdity. There are decidedly pacifistic, antiwar tendencies in both. Each utilizes the narrative framework of the adolescent love story (two in the later work), and in each case, the novelist is even more preoccupied with the postwar situations, not truly peace, but "un-war," unrecognized and mute and unfortunately unheroic.

In the more than five hundred pages of *The Dead Children* Matute pulls together and definitively enunciates many social and human problems hinted in earlier novels. The Cain theme appears in the tangled loves and hates within the family, finding maximum expression in the Civil War when two Corvos fight on opposing sides. The social tensions between rural gentry and the peasants, the decadence and disintegration of the landowning family, the unhealable differences between generations and the concomitant revolt of the young are combined with the ill-starred loves of the youngest Corvos.

The village of Hegroz in its gloomy mountain valley belonged from time immemorial to the Dukes of Hegroz, only a name for the sharecroppers and day-workers who paid forced annual tribute to the absentee landlord. One such peasant, a Corvo,[7] emigrated to America and became wealthy; his grandsons returned and bought Hegroz and its surrounding forests, building a summer house on the estate of La Encrucijada. Egotistical, voracious, indifferent to the land and its people, the Corvos were hated by the villagers. The cousins Gerardo and Elías, third generation of the new owners of Hegroz, were ruined by bank failure in Argentina where Elías, failing to salvage anything from the wreckage, shot himself. Gerardo attempted suicide by hanging from a tree in the patio but was found by Daniel (Elías' son) and saved; for the rest of his life he had a crooked neck and drank too much.

The family, now permanently installed in La Encrucijada, became progressively poorer. One year later, in 1930, Gerardo's wife Margarita died, leaving him a cowardly, inept son, César (an unsuccessful lawyer in Madrid, not a prominent figure in the novel); a vigorous, domineering nineteen-year-old daughter, Isabel, whose one amition was to reestablish the family fortunes; and a beautiful, dreamy, rebellious adolescent, Verónica. Daniel (whose mother was a mysterious Cuban, supposedly mulatto) also lived in Gerardo's house, treated as a second-class relative. Daniel, ostensible protagonist of the novel, personifies the class struggle (his mother was reputedly of the servant class), incorporating the opposing elements. His subsequent hate for the leisure class springs from his relatives' maltreatment, while his love for the poor is both instinctive and born of an awareness of injustice.

When the fourteen-year-old Verónica refused to marry a wealthy older man to repair the family fortune, Isabel arranged a marriage between Gerardo, father of both girls, and Beatriz, a moderately prosperous old maid of forty, who died within a year after giving birth to Mónica near the end of 1932. Discovering the love of Verónica and Daniel, Isabel (jealous because of a repressed love for the boy) caused Gerardo to expel him from the house. Three years later, having established himself in Barcelona and joined the Socialist Party, Daniel returned to meet Verónica, who ran away from La Encrucijada forever. Daniel joined the Republican Army during the Civil War, and in 1938, while he was in the trenches, Verónica and their unborn child were killed in an air raid (one of the "dead children" of the title). At war's close, Daniel fled to France, and was interned in a concentration camp. Later, he did forced labor in the mines, contracting an incurable respiratory disease. Broken and embittered, he returned to Hegroz in the spring of 1948, but only to work as forest ranger on the estate. He became acquainted with Diego Herrera, idealistic director of the nearby penal colony whose workers were constructing a dam. In discussions, they relived their past while trying to forget, tentatively moving toward understanding between former enemies who fought on opposing sides, an attempt, born of loneliness and despair, to overcome the bitterness left by the war.

Mónica, now sixteen, represents the younger generation. Like Verónica, whom she resembles physically and psychologically, she frequently escapes from Isabel to the woods, and so meets Miguel, a young convict, with whom she falls in love. Unlike many, Miguel was not a political prisoner, but had become involved in drug traffic in Barcelona, and was left by mature criminals to "take the rap" for them. Obsessed by freedom, Miguel escaped after killing a man, and was found in the mountains by Daniel who for a time hid him in his cabin. The latter subsequently changed his mind and forced Miguel out into woods filled with soldiers and dogs hunting him. As Daniel killed a wolf the following day, he heard another shot, signifying the death of Miguel; symbolically, the dead wolf and the corpse of Miguel are brought in at the same time. The wolf motif recurs frequently, not only in connection with Miguel, but with various groups whose normal needs and wants are frustrated: the Barcelona proletariat, the landless peasants, the rebellious Daniel in his youth, the repressed Mónica who is a "wolf cub." *The River* and *Halfway Down the Road* associate the wolf with fear and hunger, noting that the animal attacks only when driven to do so by starvation. The wolf motif was considered of such importance by the French translators that the title was changed to *Plaignez les loups (The Wolves Are Howling)*.

The novel is not unfolded in linear chronology, but uses several different, juxtaposed time sequences. The present time of the novel is 1948, after Daniel's return to Hegroz; this is alternated with flashbacks and memories (first those of Daniel, then those of Miguel), usually triggered as reactions to specific situations somehow associated with those recalled. Action in the present is concentrated in January, month of wolf hunts in the area. The juxtaposition of different times and the confrontation of age groups establish parallels in the lives and situations of the two generations (of Daniel and Verónica, Miguel and Mónica), indicating that the war really changed nothing. Past and present are the same: time is annihilated; earlier events become meaningless. The novel thus protests the useless sacrifice of a conflict where nothing essential was accomplished.

Various significant aspects of the novel are not easily summarized ("orchestration," the background and secondary characters), but these carry much of the message. It is not merely a novel of hate and love and war, but a social novel with the ever-present problem of land distribution, of absentee landlordism, dispossessed peasants and un-worked fields, of poverty, misery, and subhuman conditions on the one hand, balanced by a sterile, decadent leisure on the other. It is a novel of the forgotten villages of Castile, hopelessly ignorant and desperately limited, which make alcoholics of schoolmasters, doctors, and educated "outsiders." At the same time, it is a novel of the Barcelona proletariat, their hunger, suffering, and injustices, an impressionistic mosaic of the causes underlying the popular revolt in the Civil War. Daniel's experiences in the Republican Army reflect the optimism, bravery, and hopelessness of untrained and poorly-equipped volunteers pitted against superior training and equipment, against Mussolini's and Hitler's planes, troops, and munitions. However, Matute does not idealize the lower classes or whitewash the Republicans. She shows a sufficient number of atrocities (albeit implicitly conditioned by environment) to indicate that her message transcends partisanship. A civil war is a war that nobody wins, but the special losers are the children, as is shown through the recollections of Miguel, too young to participate other than as a spectator of the terror and a victim.

Daniel's fate at the end of the war reflects the plight of many of the vanquished: considerable numbers were still not free, and most of those working on the dam were political prisoners. *The Dead Children* is a cry for liberty, a desire for freedom by no means limited to Miguel, for whom the yearning becomes an obsession, stronger than love and stronger than death. More than a novel of war, this is a novel of its aftermath, a fact which Spanish commentators of the novel have had to overlook completely since at worst, a mention of implications might be interpreted as the critic's personal views, and at best, to point out an intention or import which the censors overlooked would be a disservice both to the novelist and the publisher. For this reason and others peculiar to the Spanish situation, the most significant criticism is not Spanish—despite the enormous publicity resulting from the two prizes—but foreign, particularly French, with various critical notices in English, German, Russian, and Swedish, and a sprinkling in several other languages.

Discussing *The Dead Children* with Alexandre Kalda,[8] Matute observed that generally soldiers neither know exactly what they are doing nor why they are doing it, for they are simple men, and the ideas, abstract. "I believe that one can speak of war without indulging in politics. It is a chapter of history . . . . With time, war is no longer an abstract myth, but a myth incarnate. There are new men, a new conscience. I wished to de-mythesize that epoch and bring it into the domain of legend . . . if I could say that I have tried to make a myth of another myth, that might be almost right. Let us say that from something mythical, I have tried to make something mythological." In her understanding of mythology, each personage plays a clearly defined role, each represents something, and lives a directly comprehensible life, a life which abruptly ceases to be quotidien and approaches the realm of the supernatural or larger-than-life.

These remarks seem to imply clearly enough that the novelist has attempted to give a symbolic value to the various characters of *The Dead Children*, a symbolism implicit in the nature of the lives of each. Considered in this light, César Corvo, Gerardo's ineffective son who fought on the Nationalist side, becomes a symbol of the *estraperlista* (black marketeer), of all the unscrupulous profiteering which characterized the postwar period of want. Even though he becomes immensely wealthy he fails to give any impression of energy or real ability; he continues to be a gray and faintly despicable figure, distinguished largely by his selfishness. Isabel, vastly more energetic, is hardly admirable, and though the novelist seems to feel some sympathy for her, she has extremely little patience with what this character represents. Certain declarations made by the novelist to Claude Couffon[9] give an explicit interpretation: "Isabel is a personage taken from reality. She represents the frequent type of Spanish woman obsessed by sin—who brandishes the Sixth Commandment[10]—and becomes hard, pitiless, demanding, terribly cruel, and inflexible towards those who have fallen into this tempting sin. Vain, proud of her virtue and secretly detesting it, Isabel has numerous models (with many variations, of course) among provincial and village women."

Verónica is purity and revolt; Mónica, dreams assassinated, shattered illusions. The Corvo (i.e., *Cuervo*, "Crow") family are predators, symbolizing the *caciques* (rural bosses) and large landowners, degenerate and nonproductive. Gerardo is hate and impotence incarnate, while Daniel, as seen in the novel's present time, is defeat; in the past he represented Republican ideals. For Mónica, Daniel is time, the past personified. In his ultimate decision to oust Miguel, sending him to almost certain death, Daniel is claudication, a surrender of ideals once uniting him with others like the young escapee. The latter is a clear-cut victim of society, from his birth in the slums and early years of deprivation, to his postwar involvement with the underworld. Miguel exemplifies environmental determinism; with his circumstances, it was almost inevitable that he should eventually end as a fugitive, felled by police bullets. At the same time, he incarnates an enormous desire to live, a thirst for life, and a hunger for freedom conveyed by the insistent wolf imagery. Diego Herrera, idealistic head of the penal colony, is a man of good will, who wishes to forget the past horrors and carry out a work of regeneration. Herrera fought in the war on the Nationalist side and lost his only son, horribly tortured by the "Red" opponents. His conversations with Daniel symbolize the necessary reconciliation between old enemies and the novelist's effort to show how past suffering should unite rather than divide. It is Herrera's phrase which gives the novel its title when he observes that the "dead children" weigh heavily upon them both.

In large part Herrera would seem to represent attitudes with which the novelist sympathizes, despite the failure of his attempt to reform

Miguel. He is one of very few in the novel who undertake any positive action (although it is clear that he is thwarted mostly by official policies hostile to his goals), and the implication is that further needless tragedy might be averted if those like Herrera had more freedom to act. The novel's primary message, however, is the futility of war, as Matute declared[11] in the previously cited interview with Claude Couffon: "Above all, I have tried to portray the useless sacrifice of a war which has changed nothing. Time weighs, unchangeable, on the characters of the book. Past and present are one and the same: time has no meaning." Everything is immobile, as in a dream. A great despair slowly eats into the heart of Daniel; he would like to salvage his own generation through Miguel, who represents youth, but it is too late. "Our children are born dead; we are a lost generation," he says, "but there is hope despite everything, through those who will come after . . . ." This is symbolized by Tañaya, a peasant woman who long before helped Verónica and Daniel, and speaks with him at the end of the novel. Those of her children whom he remembers have died, but "then there were others . . . and still more may come. That's life" (p. 557).

CHAPTER 9

The Trilogy, Los mercaderes (The Merchants)

I Recent Biography

THE PERIOD corresponding to the inception of the trilogy included difficult years for the novelist despite several literary triumphs, for her marriage, which had been increasingly unhappy, deteriorated sharply. Her mother died, Matute's personal life was "disastrous," and she suffered two serious illnesses and major surgery. Perhaps the growing elements of pessimism and melancholy which have been noted in her works[1] owe more than a little to these experiences. At the same time, the renewed prominence of works of fantasy may similarly reflect the search for refuge in the happier world of imagination.

In January of 1963, Matute was definitively separated from her husband. Divorce has never existed in Spain; the only solution to an intolerable situation is legal separation, which does not permit remarriage but does at least allow the woman to regain some legal rights lost at matrimony. During the more than two years of the legal process, the novelist lived under considerable civil and physical restriction, awaiting the verdict of the Curia.[2] After her separation, Matute began to travel with greater frequency, visiting Greece and Corfu, returning to France, and touring Belgium, Germany, and Switzerland. In the fall of 1964 she visited the United States for the first time, at the invitation of several universities, where she lectured and read from her works. The following spring, questions of legal separation were finally resolved with a favorable judgment, giving the novelist custody of her son, which permitted her to accept one of several offers and return to the United States as a visiting professor at the University of Indiana during 1965-66. Before doing so, she traveled extensively in Scandinavia, Northern, and Central Europe, her visits frequently coinciding with the release of translations of her works, which by 1965 had appeared in every Western European language except Greek, and in several of the "Iron Curtain" tongues.

Work on the final volume of the trilogy was to have been completed during the year at Indiana, but its failure to appear for some three years thereafter suggests the possibility of revisions or even extensive rewriting after the novelist's return to Spain. Upon returning home, Matute accepted another lecture tour, speaking in Salamanca, Avila, Segovia, Zamora, and other cities during the summer of 1966. Once back in Barcelona, she began to seek a home for herself and Juan Pablo, eventually settling upon the picturesque Costa Brava town of Sitges, a fashionable summer resort. She returned to the United States a third time in 1969, lecturing at the University of Oklahoma and several other American universities, but these recent years have been largely devoted to her son and her writing. "I am now entering a perfect age for writing," she recently observed, "that age of plenitude, for seeing things not too passionately. Passionately, yes; I am passionate and cannot be otherwise . . . when it is a question of injustice—but with a greater knowledge and more just criteria. It is an age when one has sufficient experience of life in order to speak of certain things, without the discouragement of age, when one feels internally filled to overflowing with life. For working it is very good."[3]

In the summer and fall of 1970, a number of politically disturbing events occurred in Spain, with notable increases in the Basque and Catalonian separatist or "nationalistic" activity. While in no sense an activist, Matute was drawn by her mounting social consciousness and political concern to join with a group of over 300 *catalán* intellectuals, artists, writers, architects, publishers and entertainers in a show of opposition to the Franco regime. Journeying individually and in small groups to the Monastery of Montserrat, they drafted a defiant text supporting the Basque nationalists and asking for numerous guarantees of public liberties and civil rights, including abolition of the death penalty. Expelled from the Monastery by the *Guardia Civil* and specially armed police, the signers were arrested, with the best known receiving heavy fines. Matute, perhaps the most famous of the writers participating, was fined 50,000 pesetas (apparently the maximum for a similar offense). This, together with the increasingly critical tone of her most recent writings, could foreshadow the adoption of a still more definite posture of opposition in the future. Her apparently tranquil withdrawal to Sitges notwithstanding, it is obvious that the final word has not been written on either Matute or her work.

II   Primera Memoria (First Memoirs)

This initial volume of the projected trilogy, *The Merchants*, was submitted under a pseudonym to the competition for the 1960 Premio Nadal, the author's identity remaining secret until after *First Memoirs* had won. The decision caused considerable controversy in Spain as this prize was originally instituted to "discover" new authors; however, a majority of the awards since 1960 have been to the unpublished novels of authors already known to the public. With this award, Matute had won all of the major Spanish novelistic prizes, and was further recognized by the Hispanic Society of America which elected her a corresponding member. *First Memoirs* was translated almost immediately to French and shortly thereafter to German, appearing as a serial in a prestigious Stuttgart daily newspaper. There were simultaneous English and American translations, respectively entitled *Awakening* and *School of the Sun*, and this novel (together with *The Dead Children*) has continued to be a favorite of critics who see it as one of Matute's most typical and significant novels.

The trilogy has no continuity of plot between its parts, but a strong unity of theme and intention. Although individual volumes may be read as complete units, the novelist observed that it is difficult to appreciate the significance of the trilogy without reading it as a whole. The title's meaning is not apparent until volume two. The "merchants" are not only those who traffic with and seek to store up material goods, but all who attempt to exploit the needs, sentiments, or ideals of others for their own benefit. The world of the *mercaderes* is not strictly the business world, but is found wherever someone takes advantage of the misfortunes, weaknesses, ignorance, or the very existence of others. In a deeper sense, it includes all who live without idealism, reducing human values to merchandise bought and sold. The "merchants," the materialists, are the majority, with only a few exalted idealists.

The Merchants continues many typical, obsessive Matute themes: the Civil War, Cain and Abel, the gulf between generations, the separate worlds of childhood and adolescence, the themes of loss, alienation, solitude, revolt, preoccupation with injustice and hypocrisy, social inequities, and most obviously, the opposition between materialism and idealism.

First Memoirs is another excellent subject for a study of Matute's style, with an extremely poetic prose which alternates long, lyrical passages with abrupt, fragmentary sentences. The unconventional use of colors, often expressionistic or surrealistic, properly lights a work whose background is war with ghostly or terrifying reflections. The plot is loose and the form autobiographical, a first-person narrative memoir composed by fourteen-year-old Matia.[4] She does not proceed in straight chronological order, nor follow a free association of ideas, but moves backward and forward in time, presenting disconnected memories, announcing what is going to happen, presenting characters bit by bit. Different time sequences are juxtaposed, as in *The Dead Children*, here constituting a "triple point of view":[5] Matia's narration of events from her adolescence; her random comments and evocations, also belonging to her adolescence, but not necessarily to the moment or events in the memoir; and present-tense comments by the older Matia at the moment of writing. Her comments and reflections, constituting a sort of interior monologue, are printed in parentheses to separate them from the retrospective action.

Matute in *First Memoirs* has abandoned the setting of her previous works for an unnamed island. Place names and those of certain characters indicate one of the Balcares; most critics have supposed that it is Mallorca.[6] The action takes place during the early part of the Civil War, which is ever present, more felt than seen. The war in the peninsula is never described and only distant echoes reach the island, but there are various wars on a smaller scale: that of the Taronji brothers (Fascists) against political undesirables on the island (including their cousin of the same name—the Cain theme, war within the family); the "war" of Doña Práxedes, Matia's grandmother, to preserve the *status quo*; and the counterpoint adolescent "war," or clashes between juvenile gangs. The use of an island, removed from the main conflict, and of child or adolescent protagonists, may be seen either as a device to circumvent censorship, or as a microcosmic, symbolic representation of the national situation.

Complementing these tensions and conflicts and an atmosphere of overt and covert hate and cruelty is the psychological anguish of Matia, her nostalgia for lost childhood, her resistance at entering the adult world which she senses is sordid and corrupt. Typically, the protagonist is an "orphan:" her mother is dead, and she feels abandoned by her father, fighting on the Republican side. The Cain theme is seen here also, as Borja's father is fighting with the Nationalists, and Matia and her cousin each identify with the cause espoused by their respective progenitors. Matia has been recently separated from her old nurse and brought against her will to live with her grandmother. She shares with the novelist a love for her puppet theater and a black doll, "Gorogó," a symbol of childhood.

Matia's tyrannical cousin Borja, one year her senior, is her only companion. This hypocritical and Machiavellian but also slightly pathetic adolescent probably personifies the "perverse innocence" which the novelist has identified as the theme of *First Memoirs*. Manuel, another important adolescent is in many ways Borja's opposite, and in others, a Christ-like figure, wrongly accused and sacrificed.[7] Betrayed by Borja and denied by Matia, Manuel is not martyred physically, but psychologically, his childhood irrevocably truncated. The transition from childhood to adulthood is a major theme, but by no means the only one, despite the fact that numerous critics (including Spanish, French, and American commentators) have given it exclusive mention. This becomes more apparent when the novel is considered in relation to other parts of the trilogy.

Various subthemes are related to this transition to adulthood: the separation and reciprocal impenetrability of the worlds of children and adults, their mutual lack of comprehension, and the adolescent's sentiment of alienation and revolt. *First Memoirs* is a tale of frustrated rebellion, nascent love, and the discovery of falseness and sordidness. The novel is divided in four parts, each involving a discovery: death, physical love (the "dirty secret of adults"), hate (war on various levels), and betrayal. As in the Garden of Eden, knowledge of good and evil brings expulsion from Paradise (childhood). The young protagonists' innocence, their cruel intolerance of human weakness in a world they neither understand nor forgive, is balanced by their egotism, spontaneous cruelty, and perversity. The roots of adult vices appear in the child, and Matia muses, "Can it be that as children we live our entire lives, and thereafter only repeat ourselves stupidly, blindly, without any meaning whatever?" (p. 20). Nonetheless, youthful cruelty has some purity and innocence when contrasted with the grandmother's hardness, the sickly blandness of Aunt Emilia (Borja's mother), the moral corruption and hypocrisy of adults in general, and the especially sinister complicity of the priest, Mossen Mayol.

The novel's significance must be sought on symbolic and psychological levels rather than in its slender plot. Matia and Borja, escaping their grandmother's vigilance to the boat "Joven Simeón," found there the corpse of José Taronji, and met Manuel, his supposed son, who came for the body. The friendship which Matia subsequently formed with Manuel (with undertones of adolescent love) annoyed Borja whose jealousy grew after learning that Manuel was the illegitimate son of Jorge de Son Major, lord of the island. Borja was enraged when this colorful adventurer ignored his idolatry, favoring Manuel, and consequently used the confessional to lie about a theft of money from his grandmother for which he blamed Manuel. The latter was sent to a reformatory while Matia, impotent and ashamed, was unable to defend Manuel or even warn him.

Lauro, "el Chino," the unfortunate ex-seminarian and tutor, sadistically tyrannized and terrorized by Borja; Antonia, Lauro's mother, abused by the grandmother; and Sanamo, slithery servant of Jorge de San Major, are—with most other secondary characters—corrupt, decaying in various strange ways. Matia herself senses a similar process as she begins to enter the world of adults, a psychological study which is undoubtedly one of Matute's best.

First Memoirs is deceptively simple, concentrating its focus on an adolescent girl and her emotional problems, and although it would deserve its high ranking solely for its contribution to adolescent psychology, it is more profound than immediately apparent, a study of war and the causes of war, those produced by the social order and those inherent in human nature—a study of social and personal corruption. In addition to the obsessive themes of Cain and Abel, adult-childhood worlds, solitude, alienation and hypocrisy, the theme of loss is very strong. This is indirectly related to the overall theme of the trilogy in the final paragraph when the obviously symbolic cock of Son Major cries out for "some mysterious lost cause" lost innocence, lost idealism, lost hope, lost Republic.

III   Los soldados lloran de noche
(The Soldiers Cry By Night)

This exceedingly tenuous continuation is not strictly a sequel, although Manuel serves as a link between the separate narratives and largely different casts of characters. Again, formal plot is minimal, with much supposedly autobiographical retrospection. Most "present-tense" action takes place in the closing months of the Civil War, a lapse of perhaps two years since the first part. As in *The Dead Children*, the past looms large. Matute utilizes a technique of alternating, crossing, and interweaving past and present, combining subjective feelings and objective events, actions, and memories. Short, informative notes on actual happenings (somewhat in the journalistic style of Dos Passos) contrast with the lengthy, retrospective, personal account of Marta. Initially the same island of *First Memoirs*, the setting is subsequently changed to the mainland. As in *In This Land*, the final, tragic scene relives the entry of Nationalist (Franco) forces into Barcelona.

Neo-realistic description is used interchangeably with interior monologue, illustrating Matute's combination of her personal brand of Objectivism with opposing poetic and psychological currents.

The novel has three divisions: *Arena (Sand)*, *Lluvia (Rain)*, *Niebla (Fog)*. In each abound rhetorical figures related to the titular noun, recurrent variations of the dominant motif. More obvious than in *First Memoirs* is the division of the cast into "merchants" (the vast majority) and "soldiers" (those few who via idealism or heightened sensitivity manage to achieve a place apart). The heroes are those capable of self-sacrifice. Symbolizing these is Jeza, a Communist organizer executed by the Nationalists, who dominates the novel without ever appearing. The vague biblical connotations of his name are reinforced by the insistent use of the phrase, "a man called Jeza." The memory of this idealist is constantly evoked in the thoughts and words of the protagonists, Manuel and Jeza's widow Marta who (without understanding Jeza or his cause) recognize something extraordinary in him. His life and death had meaning because of his devotion to a cause superior to himself (strikingly similar to Ortega's concept of the noble man). In quest of understanding the mystery of Jeza and carrying on his mission, Marta and Manuel personify a symbolic, mystic search for an ideal: modern youth's desperate striving toward something to believe in, something still untarnished and beautiful, even if wrong. "Jeza was *himself*, an affirmation." That he might be mistaken does not enter in their calculations.

At the death of Jorge de Son Major, Manuel has been recognized as his son and heir. This, however, is a source of disillusionment, another revelation of the world's falsness. The boy rejects the new social position in favor of some vague principle, subsequently searching for a meaning for his life. This quest takes him to Marta for more information about the man who had indelibly impressed him. Marta's recount of her past, prior to her "redemption" by Jeza,[8] introduces the most sordid characters and surrounding of Matute's writing: a demi-monde of narcotics and sex, abortionists and thieves. Marta's mother, interested solely in pleasure, ran a sort of boarding house, neither too clean nor too moral. To escape, and also in revenge for maternal mistreatment, Marta ran away with her mother's lover Raúl, brother of Jeza. The Cain theme reappears in the brothers' relationship and their contrasting personalities, here extended to personify extremes of materialism and idealism. Marta's decision to follow Jeza is more than a choice between two men: with something of the religious conversion, it is a choice between a life without values and a life in the service of an ideal, even if imperfectly comprehended.

Before his death, Jeza entrusted to his wife certain compromising documents for his comrades in Barcelona. Fulfilling this last wish becomes an imperative for Manuel and Marta, despite the dangers of such a mission. Under cover of fog, they travel in a small boat to the mainland and hand over Jeza's legacy. Then, assuming his destiny, they do not attempt escape or neutrality but, in the hopeless last defense of Barcelona, choose death before an advancing Fascist tank, mystically believing that dying for a cause (even though not their own) gives meaning to their lives.

While the novelist nowhere explicitly states that Jeza was a Communist, this is indicated by his activities and personality. The use of such a character as symbol of an ideal is unprecedented in postwar Spanish literature, and Matute did not expect the censors' permission. Their approval undoubtedly owes much to her numerous foreign publishing contracts; the paucity of Spanish criticism of what is obviously a major work shows clearly that the subject is still taboo. Matute's use of a Communist hero does not indicate party sympathies: Jeza is not so much a symbol of a concrete ideology as of devotion and service to an ideal. Communism may have been chosen because of the fervor of its adherents, or the almost religious dedication exacted of the party faithful.

Reinforcing the title, the atmosphere of the novel is frequently depressive, foreboding tragedy. It is filled with psychic tensions, bitterness, melancholy, and mystery. The title (from a line by Nobel Prize poet, Salvatore Quasimodo) probably suggests the essential solitude of the "soldiers" in a conflict almost inevitably won by the "merchants," the loneliness of those who try to change the world or to improve the lives of others, and who are defeated or annihilated by the opposition or sheer dead weight of materialism. The division of the world into "merchants" and "soldiers" is obviously oversimplified, but Matute thereby achieves a hauntingly powerful symbolism.

IV   La trampa (The trap)

The third and final volume of the trilogy, repeatedly announced for publication in the three years intervening between Matute's return from Indiana and the work's ultimate release in the summer of 1969, was awaited with considerable expectation. There had been various critical predictions that it would be an especially important novel; there were statements to the effect that if the last volume fulfilled the promise of the preceding two, the trilogy would be one of the most significant literary entities of the postwar years. The prolonged, unexplained delays in its appearance at first added to the expectation, but were so extended that before its release the matter was nearly forgotten. Because of this (and perhaps also because of a certain cautiousness about the censorship), extremely few critical notices of *The Trap* appeared in the first year following its publication.

The trilogy in its entirety cost Matute the better part of a decade, exactly ten years having elapsed since the completion of *First Memoirs* in 1959, and five since the release of the second volume. The individual parts of *The Merchants* have been crafted with noticeably greater care and awareness of the novelistic craft than most of Matute's earlier works, and represent a more mature and less impassioned judgment. From the technical and formal point of view, the trilogy is more complex than the writings prior to the decade of the sixties—and it should be noted that several volumes published early in this decade were written previously, then collected and reissued. This is true in particular of the short story collections, and many memoirs and chronicles. Except for the trilogy, the only work which apparently belongs entirely to this decade is *A Few Kids*, and like the trilogy, it shows evidence of longer and more careful polishing. Matute seems either to be writing less, or retaining recent works longer, refining them before publication.

The novelist's affirmation that the various parts of the trilogy, while independent, can be better understood by reading the whole, is borne out strongly by the third volume, which throws considerable light on passages of *First Memoirs* and *The Soldiers Cry*. . . . With its numerous allusions to the earlier novels and many characters from the first part who reappear without further introduction, the third novel is definitely the least independent. Some familiarity with the first part of the trilogy seems practically indispensable for comprehension of certain parts of *The Trap*. The degree of independence is greater in the case of the second volume, which in a sense constitutes a long parenthesis or digression in the story of Matia and her family, begun in the first novel and completed in the third.

The action of the first volume takes place in the early years of the Spanish Civil War (before the outcome has become predictable), that of the second in the final weeks of that same conflict, and the third is set some twenty-five to thirty years later. The setting changes from the island seen in *First Memoirs* to the mainland in the second part, and is amplified to include even a view of America in the third, but before the end, the surviving characters gather again in the same initial surround-ings, the microcosmic island. This inevitably insinuates the question as to what has changed in the meanwhile, or exactly what the Civil War and the "horrors of peace" have accomplished. The reply would seem to be that little, if anything, has changed on any really significant level. There have been superficial changes, symbolized by Borja's rather abortive, half-hearted attempts at modernizing the grandmother's house, but on a deeper level things remain unchanged (as seen in the survival of the grandmother, essentially changeless, with all she represents, and with the same old servants still in a state of near serfdom). If the first two novels may be considered, on one level, studies of the profound and all but invisible causes of the civil war—causes inherent in the social structure of the nation—the final volume of the trilogy investigates the same phenomena from the perspective of the present, discovering only slight and superficial variations.

Matia and Borja, adolescents in *First Memoirs*, reappear three decades later in *The Trap* as adults who have left youth definitively behind, albeit without really maturing, without becoming responsible or acquiring control of their own destinies. Their adult personalities are the logical extension of those seen as adolescents, and it is obvious to the reader that a continuous thread of development unites these two moments in their lives, even though the novelist omits much of the intervening period. Their lives are unfolded sufficiently in accord with their intimate psychic necessities to give the result an air of inevitability.

Structurally, *The Trap* is quite complex. Like the two previous volumes, it also has an internal division into three parts, but instead of the first-person, retrospective diary of Matia, or the vaguely parallel monologue-narratives of Manuel and Marta (in *The Soldiers Cry . . .*), *The Trap* has four narrators, consciences, or points of view, identifiable by the titles given the various chapters, and then repeated more or less haphazardly. Thus, six chapters entitled "Diario en desorden ("Disordered Diary") are narrated from within the equally disordered consciousness of Matia. "Perder el tiempo" ("Wasting Time") is the title of five chapters, four concentrated in the first part, which constitute the experience and point of view of "Bear," Matia's son. "Tres días de amor" ("Three Days of Love") is the title of six chapters whose narrative perspective is situated within the consciousness of Mario, a radical or revolutionary social activist of perhaps forty years of age. The remaining five chapters, "En esta ciudad" ("In This City"), are experienced from the vantage point of the inner subjectivity of Isabel, Mario's scheming mistress.

Although the distribution of chapters is numerically rather even, the most significant portions of the narrative belong to Matia, not merely because it is with her that the book begins and ends, but also because she alone, of the important characters, is already previously known to the reader of earlier parts of the trilogy. Then, too, the "Disordered Diary" reaches at times a truly admirable level of artistry, quite likely the best Matute has achieved to date, and often markedly superior to other parts of the novel.

The handling of time is complex, and occasionally difficult to follow, with the reader forced to jump in free-association style from present to any number of pasts. The plot is likewise diffuse, reviewing Matia's life since the end of the war, and summarizing the essential vital experiences of the other three narrative consciousnesses or perspectives, previously unknown quantities for the reader. Thus, the novel is largely retrospective, with its action internal (and hence basically static), consisting of memories and evocations of the past; however, it does include minimal external action, concentrated in some three days of the present epoch.

The principal setting is the same crumbling mansion first seen in volume one, still more decadent and yet somehow timeless, defying all attempts at modernization. Even more than the house, the characters have somehow decayed in the interim, not merely aging but de-generating. Matia has returned to the island at the imperious invitation of her grandmother, who plans a centenary celebration (though she will only be ninety-nine). Hating the old woman and the house as well, Matia is yet powerless to refuse: something compels her to respond to the summons. On this level of significance may be perceived one of the symbolic implications of the title: Matia's upbringing is a trap; the conditioning and conventions of her class are like a labyrinth. A similar significance is evident in the case of Matia's cousin Borja, an aging playboy who has long since squandered his inheritance, wasting his life in endless waiting for the grandmother's demise. In his case, the trap is baited with money, and Borja's independence and hypothetical authenticity are forfeit.

Aunt Emilia reappears, having aged relatively much more than the grandmother. Bearing in mind the old woman's identification with the ancient political system, *caciquismo* ("Bossism"), it is obviously significant that her health is so strong. Much more weakened are the aged servants, but nonetheless, they continue as always in their positions, obviously too feeble for many of the tasks before them.

It is revealed that Matia, shortly after the end of the Civil War, went to America to rejoin her father who (as a Republican) had gone into exile, obtaining a position as professor of Spanish at an American university (similar in many respects to that of Indiana, where Matute spent a year). Here Matia met David Díaz, son of a Spaniard exiled some years previously, and an extremely self-sufficient American lady, somehow connected with the academic world. The boy, product of a broken home, hypersensitive, and rather weak, is a character never too convincingly developed, although this may be the result of his appearing only via the half-smothered memories of Matia, who married him when he was called to the Army during World War II and bore his child during his absence. Whether due to war experiences or inherent weaknesses, Matia's husband returned an incipient alcoholic, and despite beginning graduate studies, rapidly deteriorated to a point where he had to be committed permanently to a sanatorium. His mother, apparently of independent means, encouraged Matia to obtain a separation and travel for a time, furnishing her money and keeping the child. Without consciously intending to do so, Matia allows this to become a permanent way of life, literally abandoning her son, and traveling endlessly in search of love and of herself, without ever finding either. When at last she faces reality, her son is an adult, and Matia's chance for meaningful existence is long past, gone without her ever having recognized the moment.

Matia's father, who is only a shadowy memory in *First Memoirs,* is here more convincing as a symbol of the exile than as a father. The novelist suggests that the grandmother deliberately undermined Matia's chances for a close relationship with her father, but at no time does that relationship show past, present, or potential meaning for either of them. What is most memorable in the father is his passion for Spain, which he both loves and hates, never returning but never forgetting, talking endlessly of Spain to his grandson, who (having little or no idea of what he wants from life) allows himself to be convinced to go to Spain to study. His entry into that country symbolizes the old man's vicarious return—but the grandfather himself watches from the French side of the border.

In Barcelona, "Bear" is tutored by Mario, a minor professor whose major activity is as head of a secret revolutionary group. The novel's central intrigue, pulling together the scattered threads of the lives of Matia, "Bear," and Mario, concerns an assassination plot. Mario convinces his group that an island politician is a "key" man, whose death is essential to the success of their movement. It is revealed through flashbacks and obsessive memories that this man was directly

responsible for the death of Mario's father in the Civil War, and Mario's
mother has lived almost exclusively since that day for revenge. What
appears to be a planned political assassination is in reality personal
vengeance with few or no ideological or social implications (a possible
indirect commentary on many of the reprisals following the close of
Spain's civil conflict).

"Bear," having joined the group, hides Mario in a seldom used area
of the grandmother's house, following his secret arrival, timed to
coincide with the centennial celebration. The only access being through
the room occupied by Matia, she becomes an accomplice (and another
level of significance of the title becomes visible. "Bear" in effect
prepares a trap for his mother by smoothing the way to her becoming
Mario's lover, which assures her cooperation, or at least her silence).
Their relationship, however, leads Mario to confess the plot to Matia,
renouncing the killing. Neither lover realizes that "Bear" has entered
the next room, hearing only that there will be no assassination, but not
why. The boy then carries out the plan Mario was to follow, without
concealing his identity. It is an almost perfectly gratuitous crime,
except that in allowing himself to be recognized, "Bear" deliberately
destroys the family's prestige, and refuses to be the continuation of his
ancestors. The final pages leave some doubt whether "Bear" escapes
from the authorities or exactly what is his fate. Matia, somewhat tardily
experiencing maternal reactions, repeats hysterically: "Bear, where are
you now?" The boy's action is an evident rejection of his mother's
family and all it represents, a negation rather than any affirmation of
principles of his own. It may also be seen as a rejection of life, which in
a larger sense is also a *trampa*, particularly for one raised as he has been,
without preparation for coping with the problems of existence.

In addition to "trap," *trampa* also means trick or deception, and in
this sense, refers to the social structure (implying that inherited
privilege, the perpetuation of inequities, and all institutions—family,
religious, political—supporting this system are likewise part of the
trampa). On another level, it may refer to the Civil War: since nothing
has really changed, the war and subsequent dictatorship, with all that
these implied, were merely "tricks" to maintain the status quo, a
victimizing of the Spanish people.

As psychological probing and presentation, *The Trap* is also
outstanding. The sections narrated by the two female figures are
superior in this respect to those presented from the point of view of the
two male consciousnesses, although all four are convincing studies of
motivation. Probably because of the attention given the psyches of the

four narrative consciousnesses, most of the other characters suffer by comparison. Borja and the grandmother, who emerge as distinct and memorable figures in the first novel of the trilogy, are here reduced to rather pallid shadows of themselves, retaining importance only on the symbolic level. No other characters, despite a rather large and varied cast, emerge as individuals, functioning almost exclusively as symbols, stereotypes, and stage dressing.

Without any doubt, *The Trap* is an unusually significant novel, and one of Matute's most important works. The trilogy as a whole may well be her masterpiece; to date, only *The Dead Children* can be compared with it. But *The Trap* is also at times a rather uneven novel. While perhaps this would not bother the Spanish audience (for whom, after all, the novel is intended), there are a few minor false notes in the passages relating Matia's stay in the United States, miniscule anachronisms which may distract the American reader and detract from more important aspects of the novel. Then, too, the five chapters relating the experience and vital perspective of Isabel do not seem generically or artistically necessary, despite their thematic relevance, and at times seem almost to interrupt further a continuity already fragmented by the frequent shifts of time and place and the use of multiple consciousnesses and points of view. On the other hand, the sections relating Matia's stay in the States should not be considered a total error, inasmuch as it is abundantly evident (when considered in relation to the trilogy's overall structure) how appropriate is the inclusion of a figure representative of the Republican exiles. And these minor objections aside, the rest of the novel contains many truly admirable pages, with the "Disordered Diary" of Matia unquestionably among the best of Matute any time, anywhere.

CHAPTER 10

Summation

WHEN THE Spanish Civil War ended in 1939, many of the great writers and intellectual leaders of the prewar period had vanished from the literary scene. Unamuno and Valle-Inclán were dead, Lorca assassinated, Antonio Machado dead (due partly to the rigors of his flight into exile). Pérez de Ayala and Ortega had left the country, their voices silenced for all practical purposes, and would never again be recognized as rallying points or moving forces. Rafael Alberti, Pedro Salinas, Luis Cernuda, and many other poets of the "Generation of 1927" had gone into exile; Miguel Hernández was to die soon after in a Falangist prison. Those of the previous generation who chose to remain in Spain, or returned after a brief period, such as Baroja and Azorín, never again became effective, recognized leaders, nor were they associated in any way with literary innovation. Dozens of other writers, many of whose names were almost as well known as those just mentioned, left Spain for prolonged or permanent absences.

The years immediately following the conflict were of necessity poor in intellectual and literary activity; it remained for a new generation to develop and fill the void. Glimmerings of literary revival came in the early forties, with the first novels of Camilo José Cela and Carmen Laforet, soon to be followed by a host of others. The succeeding quarter century has seen a veritable fever of activity in the drama, poetry, and the novel, to the extent that many critics have spoken of a postwar "Renaissance." Considering the size of the country and the percentage of its population which might statistically be expected to be aspiring writers, the quantity of novelistic production can only be called unprecedented. Eugenio G. de Nora's study of contemporary novelists (1962)[1] covered a selected group of over two hundred new novelists who had first published after the war, and this listing by no means exhausts the would-be producers of the genre. Over three hundred manuscripts were entered in the judging for a recent Premio

144

Nadal, and while most remain unpublished and consigned to probably well-deserved oblivion, some idea of the amount of writing in progress can be obtained, particularly if it is remembered that besides the Nadal, there are some forty other national prizes in the field of the novel (without counting other genres, and bearing in mind that the prizes awarded by provinces and municipalities are legion).

With a country like Spain, whose literature has until rather recently been all but unknown beyond its linguistic and cultural boundaries, it is difficult to place its writers in a meaningful perspective, and more particularly so on the international level. It is curious that no Spanish novelist has received a Nobel Prize; the name of Pérez Galdós (now considered by most critics as an equal of Balzac and Dickens) was proposed, but for a variety of reasons, some political and nearly all extraliterary, the prize was not awarded to him. While it is still totally hypothetical, a group of critics has begun to suggest the name of Matute as a possible contender for the Nobel Prize in the not too distant future. This is worth mention in passing, because regardless of how hypothetical the chances of such an award, it does help to clarify Matute's standing for certain readers, and to suggest another possible perspective which will help those less familiar with the modern Spanish literary world to adjust their sense of proportion.

The quantity of writing being turned out at present in Spain continues to be impressive. One of the more recent studies, Antonio Iglesias Laguna's *Treinta años de novela española* (1938–1968),[2] studies more than 270 novelists supposedly of some significance who have written in this thirty-year period. While much of the novelistic production is mediocre, and some downright bad, a surprising amount can compare favorably with the best written in other periods of Spain's literary history. Perhaps a dozen narrators of the postwar years deserve to be considered very, very good. Few critics would coincide one hundred percent in their selection of the top five or ten, but all would include Camilo José Cela, Miguel Delibes, and Ana María Matute among the most significant. If native and foreign Hispanists were asked to name the most important female novelist of Spain today (in a period when there is an unprecedented number of productive women novelists), the selection of Matute would be all but unanimous.

Matute's work is multifaceted, but its two extremes and most frequently represented variants are the stories of fantasies and the works whose theme or background involves either the Civil War or the Castilian peasant. Her interest in this is constant, lifelong, as shown by the study of her work from the earliest preserved juvenilia and her writings of pre-adolescence, up to the latest publications. Despite certain changes or modification in her evolution as a writer, Matute's style has always been extremely personal and subjective, dominated by a primarily lyric vision of reality, or a deceptively childlike conception. Beginning with a fairly traditional structure, Matute has gradually tended to ever greater experimentation with the novelistic architecture, point of view, and treatment of time. The importance of formal plot, never a major element in her novels, has decreased, while the novelist's interest in psychology (a constant in her work) has grown ever stronger, with special emphasis on the problems of motivation, and an almost obsessive interest in the key formative factors and experiences which make people "what they are" such as the half-buried childhood trauma which may suddenly erupt in an apparently inexplicable act of adult violence.

There is a rather obvious relation between this novelistic pre-occupation and Matute's own personal obsession with the Civil War. As detailed in earlier chapters, a knowledge of Matute's personal experiences and emotional reactions in the Civil War is all but indispensable to fully understanding her work, and acquaintance with the description and circumstances of the Castilian countryside is equally important for appreciating other key facets of her novels and short stories. While none of Matute's novels are autobiographical in the strictest sense, she has written almost nothing which is not directly based upon personal experience and set in environments thoroughly familiar to her.

Matute's treatment of the child and adolescent is certainly the outstanding achievement of her characterization, with most adult figures paling by comparison. Adult and children's worlds are entirely separate and for the most part impenetrable or mutually incomprehensible. The typical Matute character is the solitary, isolated child or adolescent, often handicapped either physically, socially, or mentally (orphans, sick and abnormal children abound). Closely seconding this type is the rebellious youngster, who for any number or variety of reasons, usually feels closer to—and more accepted by—the lower strata of society, or the society of outcasts.

Matute continues to be intrigued with time, both as a theme and as a narrative possibility, being apparently particularly fascinated with the "threshold" moment or experience (of passage from childhood to adolescence, or adolescence to adulthood). At the same time, there is some experimentation with the contrary possibility, the unreality of time, and the possibilities of its annihilation. Likewise, (and more frequently of late), the reader encounters factors which render meaningless the passage of hours, days, and years. A key motif, Cain and Abel, is obviously related to two of the previously mentioned obsessive concerns, social conflict and the Civil War (often symbolized by the violence between brothers). It may well be significant that in the early works, this conflict is almost inseparable from the soil; later it becomes (by implication) more closely related to other means of production. Matute is far from being either an ideologist or thesis novelist; in fact, it would be difficult to find anything resembling doctrine or dogma in any of her works, aside from such thoroughly Christian formulas as "Love one another." Her idea of charity, as noted earlier, is much broader than simple alms-giving, and extends to many areas of human relationships, but especially to the concept of equal rights of all to the necessities of life, and to be treated with dignity and justice. Matute is sufficiently fair in her treatment of the Civil War that, even though by family, background, upbringing, and class contacts she should belong to the Nationalist (or Franco) faction, her implicit sympathies are with the vanquished, with the poor and suffering of all creeds, and with all whose rights and liberties are curtailed. Her concept of true Christianity, as expressed in "Love thy brother," implies acceptance, understanding, and sharing. To most observers, it would seem that there can be nothing tendentious or censurable in her message, yet it must be remembered that her works have nonetheless occasionally been censored.

Bearing in mind the political, social, and extra-literary factors which make it difficult to judge Matute strictly in terms of her own literary aspirations and the social demands under which they were written, it seems unfair to judge her in terms of the expectations generally held regarding young writers in other periods and other lands, even though such expectations have evolved considerably. Judging her in relation to her own aims and evaluations, it must be remembered that she believes that, in a very real sense, she is just entering her most significant period as a writer. Therefore, even though with her recently completed trilogy Matute seems to have reached a high point in her career, and even though she is riding a crest of popularity with critics and public, the literary historian must reserve final judgment for some years longer.

Notes and References

Chapter One

1. Ana María Matute, *El tiempo* (Barcelona: Mateu, 1963), pp. 119–20. The translation is mine, as are all those that follow unless indicated otherwise.

2. Ana María Matute, "Notas de una escritora," *Boletín* 11, Instituto de Estudios Norteamericanos, Barcelona, Spring, 1965, 5.

3. The collection of original Matute manuscripts (typescript and holograph) belonging to the Mogar Library of Boston University includes the following:

   a. "Fantasías," an original manuscript done at age five, sixteen pages with color drawings.

   b. "Figuras geométricas," an original manuscript dated 1936, twenty-one pages with drawings by Miss Matute.

   c. "Cuentos de niños," an undated original manuscript, holograph with color drawings, eighteen pages.

   d. "Alegoría primera," original manuscripts of children's tales, fifty-one pages with color drawings, dated 1938.

   e. *La revista de Shybil*, several "issues" of the children's magazine founded by Miss Matute during the Civil War; probable dating 1938. Original manuscript holograph, drawings in pencil and in color, 365 pages.

   f. "El hijo de la luna," original manuscript, holograph, ninety-two pages with color drawing, undated.

   g. "Volflorindo o los mundos ignorados," original manuscript, one notebook and loose pages with color drawings, signed 1938.

   h. "Lucecitas de plata," original manuscript, holograph with drawings, one sketch dated 1940.

   i. *Cumbres*, in play form, seventy-nine pages, mimeograph and typescript, undated.

   j. *Pequeño teatro* original manuscript, holograph, in spiral notebook, of first novel composed; 211 pages.

   k. *Los Abel* original manuscript, holograph with sections of typescript, of first novel published.

1. *El polizón del "Ulises,"* original manuscript, typescript with holograph corrections of recent prizewinning children's book. Barcelona, 1964; ninety-three pages.

Excepting the last three, these items are unpublished juvenilia. The final item, of particular interest to the scholar of contemporary Spain, is the original manuscript of:

Las luciérnagas typescript and holograph, 376 pages with Censor's stamp on frontispiece; 1949–1953. Comparison of the prohibited original with the altered second version, *En esta tierra,* could offer rich insights into the possible and impossible on the Spanish literary scene during the 1950's.

All quotations from unpublished works refer to this collection.

4. "Notas de una escritora," p. 6.

5. *Ibid.*

6. Interview by the present author with Matute, New York, September, 1965.

7. Matute, *Historias de la Artámila* (Barcelona: Destino, 1961), p. 62.

8. "Notas de una escritora."

9. Interview cited above.

10. Some examples are preserved among the juvenilia.

Chapter Two

1. Letter by Ana María Matute to the present author, January 13, 1965.

2. Matute, "A Wounded Generation," *The Nation* (November 29, 1965). Translated by A. Gordon Ferguson.

3. Matute, letter of January 13, 1965.

4. "El destino," short story in *Revista de Shybil,* No. 2 (June 1937), contains this observation: "As happiness is not lasting, so it was not for Fred." Many similar remarks could be cited.

5. This is the subject of a doctoral dissertation by Margaret E. Weitzner, *"The Novelistic World of Ana María Matute: A Pessimistic Vision of Life,* (The University of Wisconsin, 1963).

6. "A Wounded Generation," p. 29.

7. Matute, letter of January 13, 1965.

8. "A Wounded Generation," p. 29.

9. *Ibid.*

10. Most students of contemporary Spanish literature will probably associate this phrase with García Lorca, and Matute's prior acquaintance with at least some part of Lorca's work has been established. Rather than a case of influence or imitation, however, it seems more likely that both might have taken the words from a traditional Spanish song in which the refrain occurs, particularly in view of the fact that

Lorca did his own versions and arrangements of many folk songs, and because the context in which Matute uses the refrain also suggests the folk song.

11. Matute, *Cumbres*, unpublished typescript manuscript, p. 12.

12. *Ibid.*, p. 28.

13. This story later reappeared in print as part of the collection, *El tiempo*. There seems to be no relation between it and the unpublished juvenile narrative of the same name in the manuscript of *Cuentos*.

14. "A Wounded Generation," p. 31.

15. *Ibid.*

16. "Notas de una escritora," p. 11.

17. Interview by the present author with Ana María Matute, New York, September 6, 1965.

Chapter Three

1. Interview with the present author, New York, September, 1965.

2. George Wythe, "The World of Ana María Matute," *Books Abroad* XL, No. 1 (Winter, 1966), 19.

3. Matute, "A Wounded Generation," *The Nation* (November 29, 1965). Translated by A. Gordon Ferguson.

4. Subsequently published in the collection, *El tiempo*.

5. R. E. de Goicoechea, born in 1922, is the author of *Dinero para morir* (Barcelona: Mateu, 1958); *Memorias sin corazón* (Barcelona: Borrás, 1959); and *El pan mojado* (Barcelona: Pareja y Borrás, 1958). His works have been generally classified as belonging (at least in part) to the Social Realist movement.

6. Eusebio García Luengo, "Ramón Eugenio de Goicoechea y su novela, *Dinero para morir,*" *Indice*, Vol. XIII, Nos. 116–17, (September- October, 1958), 28.

7. *Ibid.*

Chapter Four

1. Interview by the present author with Matute, New York, September 5, 1965.

2. *Ibid.*

3. George Wythe, "The World of Ana María Matute," *Books Abroad*, XL, No. 1 (Winter, 1966), 19.

4. *La novela española contemporánea* (Madrid: Guadarrama, 1961), pp. 293–94.

5. Juan Luis Alborg, *Hora actual de la novela española* (Madrid: Taurus, 1958), pp. 183–84.

6. For a treatment of the *commedia dell'arte* motif in *Pequeño teatro* and a discussion of the equivalences between characters in the novel and stock types of the *commedia dell'arte*, see J. W. Díaz, "La

commedia dell'arte en una novela de Ana María Matute," in the September, 1970, issue of *Hispanófila* (no. 40; pp. 15–28).
    7. *Pequeño teatro* (Barcelona: Planeta, 1954), p. 30.
    8. *Ibid.*, p. 33.

Chapter Five

1. Typescript of *Las luciérnagas*, "Fundación Ana María Matute," Boston University Library, p. 170.
    2. The younger brother, Daniel, might also be considered a victim of his environment (especially the poverty and broken home), as he becomes the leader of a gang of delinquents. A pathetic but at the same time repulsive figure, he is totally alone emotionally and believes in nothing. Daniel dies too early in the narrative to acquire the clearly symbolic dimensions of the two older brothers.
    3. Pío Baroja's famous novel, *El árbol de la ciencia* (*The Tree of Knowledge*) presents a young physician in a similar situation, portrayed in still more sarcastic and condemnatory tones, but does not make an activist revolutionary of his protagonist.
    4. *Las luciérnagas*, p. 376.
    5. *Ibid.*, p. 165.

Chapter Six

1. First published separately, "Los cuentos, vagabundos" has subsequently appeared as the final selection in *El tiempo*.
    2. Originally published in 1956 by Ediciones Arión, Madrid, this little book rapidly became a collector's item, and has long been of lamentably limited access. Recently reissued by Destino (Barcelona, 1971), the collection is now available in an illustrated edition.
    3. *El tiempo* was first published in 1957 by Editorial Mateu (Barcelona) and reissued by them in 1963, which the Destino edition erroneously notes as the first. Destino's 1966 edition is a superior job of printing, and will probably soon be the only edition available.
    4. *La pequeña vida*, "La novela del sábado," Madrid, Ediciones Cid, is undated, and might have appeared in separate form after publication of the same novelette as the title story in the collection *El tiempo*.
    5. Barcelona: Ediciones Destino, 1961.
    6. Part of the collection has been published in a student's edition in this country. Manuel and Gloria Durán's *Doce historias de la Artámila de Ana María Matute* (New York: Harcourt, Brace and World, Inc., 1965) contains a selection of twelve of these tales, with notes, vocabulary, and supplementary questions.
    7. *El arrepentido* was first published by Editorial Rocas (Barcelona) in 1961, and soon went out of print. This edition has not been available for examination. A collection published in 1967 by Editorial Juventud

(Barcelona) with the same title is listed by that publisher as the first edition. There seems to be substantial difference in the contents of the two editions. "The Novelistic World of Ana María Matute: A Pessimistic Vision of Life," Margaret E. Weitzner's 1963 doctoral dissertation for the University of Wisconsin, mentions nine titles (pp. 48–50), two of which are omitted from the Juventud edition. Her brief discussion of the content suggests that these stories have been eliminated altogether from the collection, rather than appearing under changed titles as happened with *La pequeña vida*. Assuming that this source mentions all of the stories included in the version consulted, the more recent edition contains four stories not found in the earlier edition, which in turn included two, "El ombustero" ("The Deceiver"), ("little boy who flew with the help of an angel"), and "Mañana" ("Tomorrow")' ("in which a disillusioned crook is redeemed by the sacrifice of himself on Christmas day"), subsequently excluded. It is theoretically possible, therefore, to postulate six or more years' difference in composition dates for the various stories.

8. Margaret W(eitzner) Jones, "Religious Motifs and Biblical Allusions in the Works of Ana María Matute," *Hispania*, LI, No. 3 (September, 1968, 421.

9. Weitzner, *loc. cit.*, quotes a remark by the doctor to the effect that Miss Vivian is a somnambulist because she has a "great desire to be, and to make others, happy" which has been edited out of the later published version, probably by Matute, with the result that the story gains considerably in subtlety and undergoes a healthy decrease in sentimentalism.

10. Apparently not included in the 1961 collection, this story was published separately in *Cuadernos del Congreso por la libertad de la Cultura* No. 67 (December, 1962), with the title, "Yo no he venido a traer la paz" ("I Have Come Not to Bring Peace"). There seem to be no textual variations between the two except for the difference in titles.

11. Jones, *op. cit.*, p. 422.

12. *Ibid.*

Chapter Seven

1. For a more extensive treatment of this idea, see Janet Winecoff [Díaz], "Style and Solitude in Ana María Matute," *Hispania*, XLIX, No. 1 (March, 1966), 61–69.

2. Matute's use of color in various novels has been studied by Celia Barretini in "Ana María Matute, la novelista pintora," *Cuadernos hispanoamericanos* XLVIII, 144 (December, 1961), 405–12. The approach is mostly quantitative; without adducing many implications, she tabulates the predominant colors in the novels up to *Primera memoria*.

3. In an interview with the present author (New York, September, 1965), Matute stated that she did not consciously and deliberately select and combine rhetorical ingredients, but proceeded largely on the basis of intuition.

4. For example, Margaret Weitzner [Jones], "The Novelistic World of Ana María Matute," Ph.D. dissertation, University of Wisconsin, 1963; and George Wythe, "The World of Ana María Matute," *Books Abroad*, XL, No. 1 (Winter, 1966), 17—28.

5. Review of *Fête au Nord-ouest* by "M.M." in *Figaro Littéraire* (May 20, 1961).

6. Barcelona: Destino, 1961.

7. This observation is found in R. Vázquez Zamora's review of *Tres y un sueño* in *Destino*, June 17, 1961.

8. Barcelona: Editorial Lumen, 1961.

9. Barcelona: Editorial Argos, 1963.

10. Barcelona: Editorial Rocas, 1961.

11. Barcelona: Editorial Molino, 1961.

12. Barcelona: Editorial Garbo, 1960.

13. Barcelona: Editorial Lumen, 1965. This work won a national prize for children's literature, much to Matute's delight. She believes she has been able to help call attention to the need for a. sweeping change in juvenile fiction in Spain.

14. Barcelona: Editorial Lumen, 1960. This work was translated to French as *Le Criquet D'or* (Brussels: Gastermann).

15. Barcelona: Editorial Lumen, 1962. An English version was to be published by Pantheon (New York).

Chapter Eight

1. Luis Martín Santos, professional psychiatrist and amateur writer, was a perspicacious literary observer and a talented novelist in his own right. He was killed in an automobile accident in 1964.

2. Interview by the present author with Ana María Matute, New York, September 6, 1965.

3. *Ibid.*

4. *Ibid.*

5. Barcelona: Planeta, 1958. There are British and American versions of *The Lost Children* (published in New York by Macmillan, 1965), as well as translations to French, Czech, and Russian.

6. Within the first four or five years, *Fiesta al noroeste* was translated to French, Italian, Norwegian, Swedish, and Danish; *Los niños tontos* to German and Italian; *Pequeño teatro* and *El tiempo* to French; *Tres y un sueño* to French and English (New York: Pantheon, 1965), and *Primera memoria* to French, Portuguese, German, Swedish, Dutch, Czech, Russian, Norwegian, and English (published in New York by

Pantheon Books with the title of *Awakening*). *Los soldados lloran* ... was translated almost immediately to French, German, Czech, Russian, and Swedish.

7. The name "Hegroz," invented by Matute, is explained by Aquilino Duque in his review of *Los hijos muertos* in *Cuadernos hispanoamericanos*, XLVII, 124 (April, 1960), 148–53): " ... a horrible name suggesting atrocious aridity, saddened by plague and drought, bad wine and manure heaps, [evoking] black Christs and shrouds. ..."

8. *Arts* (April 17–23, 1963).

9. Review of *Plaignez les Loups* in *Les Lettres Françaises* (June 5, 1963).

10. In the Catholic numbering (which would be Matute's frame of reference), this commandment prohibits lust.

11. Such declarations could not be made openly in Spain, and the novel's import was particularly dangerous for several years afterward, as the Franco revolt continued to be called the "Glorious National Crusade." To imply it had accomplished nothing required integrity and courage.

Chapter Nine

1. This is the conclusion of Margaret E. Weitzner [Jones] in her doctoral dissertation, "The Novelistic World of Ana María Matute: A Pessimistic Vision of Life" (The University of Wisconsin, 1963). In what is undoubtedly the most thorough study of Matute to date, the critic points to a pessimism which grows with time, becoming increasingly evident in the later works, and in proportion to the age of a character.

2. The Curia is the body of the Catholic Church which rules on questions of separation and awards the custody of children.

3. Interview of Matute by the present author, New York, September, 1965,

4. This unusual name, a possible invention of the author's, has led certain critics to assert that Matía *is* Matute and that the novel is an autobiography, which the novelist has roundly denied. She stated in an interview with the present author (September, 1965) that *"Primera memoria* is the *least* autobiographical of my works." It is almost the only one not to use a more familiar setting.

5. Weitzner [Jones], *op. cit.* has called attention to this triple perspective, pointing out its effectiveness in obliging the reader to adopt the narrator's point of view.

6. This is initially the setting of the second novel of the trilogy which George Wythe (*op. cit.*) in an otherwise fine article has wrongly identified as the Basque fishing village of Zumaya, whence it would

have been impossible to travel as Manuel did to Barcelona.

7. The possible name symbolism is obvious; other parallels have been noted by Margaret W. Jones in "Religious Motifs and Biblical Allusions in the Works of Ana María Matute" (*Hispania*, LI, No. 3) and by Wythe (*op. cit.*).

8. The term is that of Jones *(Ibid.)*.

Chapter Ten

1. *La novela española contemporánea* (Madrid: Gredos, 1962).

2. Madrid: Editorial Prensa Española, 1969. This is an extensive study, but quite arbitrary in its selections, and most uneven in its coverage and emphasis, so that its use can be recommended only to persons thoroughly familiar with the field. In any other case, it could be seriously misleading.

Selected Bibliography

PRIMARY SOURCES

1. Ana María Matute's published writings, arranged in chronological order. (Novels are marked with an asterisk).

Los Abel (Barcelona: Destino, 1948).

Pequeño teatro (Barcelona: Editorial Planeta, 1954).

En esta tierra (Barcelona: Editorial Exito, 1955).

"La pequeña vida," *La novela del sábado* (Madrid), I, 11 (undated, but perhaps prior to 1957 when it appeared with changed title in collection *El tiempo*).

Los niños tontos (Madrid: Ediciones Arión, 1956).

El tiempo (Barcelona: Editorial Mateu, 1957. Also Barcelona: Ediciones Destino, 1966).

Los hijos muertos (Barcelona: Editorial Planeta, 1958).

"La mujer y la literatura," *Revista de actualidades, artes y letras*, VII, 217 (May 10–16, 1958).

Fiesta al noroeste (Barcelona: Pareja y Borrás, 1959. Also Barcelona: Destino, 1963).

"Autocrítica de *Fiesta al noroeste*," *Correo literario* (Barcelona), III, 46.

Paulina, el mundo y las estrellas (Barcelona: Editorial Garbo, 1960).

Primera memoria (Barcelona: Ediciones Destino, 1960).

A la mitad del camino (Barcelona: Editorial Rocas, 1961).

El arrepentido (Barcelona: Editorial Rocas, 1961).

Historias de la Artámila (Barcelona: Ediciones Destino, 1961).

Libro de juegos para los niños de los otros (Barcelona: Editorial Lumen, 1961).

El país de la pizarra (Barcelona: Editorial Molino, 1961).

Tres y un sueño (Barcelona: Editorial Destino, 1961).

Caballito loco (Barcelona: Editorial Lumen, 1962).

"Yo no he venido a traer la paz . . . ," *Cuadernos del congreso por la libertad de la cultura*, No. 67 (December, 1962).

El río (Barcelona: Editorial Argos, 1963).

Los soldados lloran de noche (Barcelona: Ediciones Destino, 1964).

El polizón del "Ulises" (Barcelona: Editorial Lumen, 1965).
Algunos muchachos (Barcelona: Ediciones Destino, 1969).
*La trampa (Barcelona: Ediciones Destino, 1969).
*La torre vigía (Barcelona: Editorial Lumen, 1971).

SECONDARY SOURCES

ALBORG, JUAN LUIS. *Hora actual de la novela española* (Madrid:
    Taurus, 1958), I, 181—90. Based primarily on *Los Abel, Pequeño
    teatro*, and *En esta tierra*, this study is particularly critical of
    what are considered rhetorical excesses of Matute.
BARRETINI, CELIA. "Ana María Matute, la novelista pintora,"
    Cuadernos hispanoamericanos, XLVIII, 144 (December, 1961),
    405—12. A survey, more quantitative than qualitative, of
    Matute's use of color in the novels up to and including *Primera
    memoria*, by the author of a less accessible work on Matute's
    treatment of children, "Los niños en la obra de Ana María
    Matute," *Universidad de Antioquia*, No 153 (2nd trimester,
    1963), 134.
CANO, JOSÉ LUIS. "Una novela de Ana María Matute, *Insula*, XIX,
    214 (September, 1964), 8—9. Excellent review of *Los soldados
    lloran de noche* and remarks on the remainder of the trilogy by a
    perceptive critic who has also reviewed for *Insula* several other
    Matute works: *Los Abel*, IV, 38 (February, 1959), 5; *Pequeño
    teatro* X, III (March, 1955), 6; *Los hijos muertos*, XIV, 146
    (January, 1959), 8—9; and *Primera memoria*, XV, 161 (April,
    1960), 8—9.
"La cárcel de papel. Sentencia dictada contra Ana María Matute," *La
    codorniz* (Madrid, June 5, 1960). Anonymous and amusing satire
    exaggerating some aspects of Matute's style, with examples taken
    largely from *Primera memoria*.
COUFFON, CLAUDE. "Una joven novelista, Ana María Matute,"
    Cuadernos hispanoamericanos, XLIV, 143 (November, 1961),
    52—55. A superior article, based on interviews and studies by the
    eminent French Hispanist; particularly useful for biographical
    factors in Matute's work.
DUQUE, AQUILINO. "*Los hijos muertos*," *Cuadernos hispano-
    americanos*, XLII, 124 (April, 1960), 148—53. Comments by an
    intelligent Spanish critic, albeit not entirely free to interpret at
    will in his review of Matute's longest novel.
"Encuesta sobre la novela contemporánea," *Cuadernos americanos*,
    XXIX, 4 (July-September, 1963), 229. Responses found on
    nearby pages by various other contemporary novelists help to
    understand Matute in relation to her colleagues and their varying
    views of the novelist's mission and craft.
FERRER, OLGA P. "Las novelistas españolas de hoy," *Cuadernos*

americanos, (Año XX), CXVIII, No. 5 (September-October, 1961), 211–23. Remarks of a sometimes arbitrary observer, but one generally admiring of Matute. The article helps to relate Matute to other presentday female Spanish novelists.

GULLÓN, RICARDO. "The Modern Spanish Novel," trans. D. M. Rogers, *Texas Quarterly,* IV, 1 (Spring, 1961), 79–96. While largely unrelated to Matute, this study offers valuable background on the Spanish novel in this century and presents a context in which her work can be better understood and evaluated.

JONES, MARGARET W(EITZNER). "Antipathetic Fallacy: The Hostile World of Ana María Matute's Novels," *Kentucky Foreign Language Quarterly,* XIII (Supplement), 1967. An excellent study of Matute's distortion of nature, particularly in imagery related to the sun and flowers in *Fiesta al noroeste, Los hijos muertos,* and *Primera memoria.*

————. Religious Motifs and Biblical Allusions in the Works of Ana María Matute," *Hispania,* LI, No. 3 (September, 1968), 416–23. A particularly useful and insightful article.

MARTÍNEZ PALACIOS, JAVIER. "Una trilogía novelística de Ana María Matute," *Insula,* XX, 219 (February, 1965), 1, 6. One of very few works on the trilogy; insightful, but cautiously worded.

NORA, EUGENIO G. DE. *La novela española contemporánea (1927–1960)* (Madrid: Editorial Gredos, 1962), II, ii. Probably the most thorough and knowledgeable coverage of the Spanish novel for the period studied, Nora's work is helpful for trends, literary fashions, and intellectual background. The section on Matute is based largely on novels up to *Primera memoria.*

NUÑEZ, ANTONIO. "Encuentro con Ana María Matute," *Insula,* XX, 219 (February, 1965), 7. Largely subjective and informal, this article nevertheless offers insights into Matute's personality.

QUINTO, JOSÉ MARÍA DE. "El mundo de Ana María Matute," *Revista española,* I, 3 (September–October, 1953), 337–41. One of the most understanding evaluations of the earlier works.

SOUCHÈRE, ELENA DE LA. *"Préface"* to *Fête au Nord-Ouest* (Paris: Gallimard, 1961), pp. 8–36. An excellent and frank study by one of Matute's translators (in French). This covers the Spanish situation particularly well.

VILANOVA, A. *"Los mercaderes* de Ana María Matute," *Destino,* (October 4–12, 1964). Somewhat inaccessible, but a commendable study of the trilogy, *Los Mercaderes,* by one of Spain's best-informed critics.

WEITZNER (JONES), MARGARET E. "The Novelistic World of Ana María Matute: a Pessimistic Vision of Life," Ph. D. dissertation, University of Wisconsin, 1963. Available through University Microfilms, Inc., Ann Arbor, Michigan, the study was published

(1970) by the University of Kentucky Press, with the title, "The World of Ana María Matute." Not available when the present manuscript was prepared, the published version contains some revisions and updating.

WINECOFF, JANET. "Style and Solitude in the Works of Ana María Matute, *Hispania*, XLIX, 1 (March 1966), 61–69. This article calls attention in particular to the alienation and solitude of Matute's characters.

WINECOFF DÍAZ, JANET. "Autobiographical Elements in the Works of Ana María Matute," *Kentucky Romance Quarterly*, (Spring, 1970). A somewhat more detailed analysis than offered by the present book of the relationship between fact and fiction in Matute's works.

——————. "*La commedia dell'arte* en una novela de Ana María Matute," *Hispanófila*, (no. 40 1970), pp. 15–28. Almost exclusively a study of *Pequeño teatro* and the way in which Matute has used elements of the puppet theater and *Commedia dell'arte* in the novel, interweaving reality, fantasy, and stylization.

WYTHE, GEORGE. "The World of Ana María Matute," *Books Abroad*, XL, No. 1 (Winter, 1966), 17–28. Generally a very good article, especially for geographical backgrounds and such general aspects as basic themes, dualisms, and use of biblical citations.

Index